Zou Zou's Story

by

Elizabeth Jane Bartholomew Spiller

2024

Dedicated to all who knew her

especially Gilbert, John, Peter and Michael

and to those who weren't lucky enough to know her.

'Zou Zou'

My mother's family were English. They lived in grand houses where they enjoyed tiffin at noon and tea at four o'clock and went to cocktail parties in the evening. They celebrated Saint George on the 23rd April with parties and flags and spoke of Home. Although *Home* was England, *home* was China and Japan.

Grandfather was 'in shipping'. He was an accountant and dealt with stocks and shares. He worked for Butterfield and Swire, known as the Blue Funnel Line from the livery of the steamers. In many major Chinese cities in those days there was a "British Concession" which often looked like a European town with Georgian and Victorian style buildings. Lionel's work was at the "Bund" – the quay – where there were "go-downs" – warehouses for goods.   He was the son of William Howell and Laura Harrington whose family had run a mineral water business based in Southend in Essex.

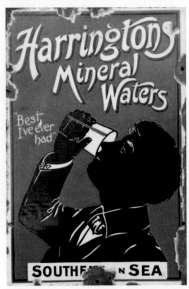

Grandmother was the second daughter of a well-to-do artist and architect, John Smedley, whose work graced Sydney, Tokyo, Hankow, Shanghai and many other eastern cities. She never considered herself Australian although she was third generation there, having been born in a house called "Uyeno", designed by her father, on "Smedley's Point" in Manly. The family left Australia for Japan when she was nine, and three years later moved to China where she was to spend the greater part of her life. However, Grandmother Gwen was staunchly English!

Gwen Smedley and Lionel Howell married on 1st June 1905 in Shanghai.

The picture shows Gwen on her wedding day.

Gwen and Lionel's lives are perhaps a different story; this one concerns their children.

Their first child, Dulcie Gwen, was born on the 5th March 1907 on a rare sojourn in England visiting Howell relations in Essex. Later in that year they returned to Kyoto and took up residence in Yokahama.

Dulcie grew to be a healthy, sensible girl, clever, industrious and a credit to the family.

Dulcie
aged 7

by her aunt
Gladys Denham

The second child was born in Japan on the 27th February 1909 in Yokahama. It was expected to be a boy and, in the Howell tradition, was to be called William. When she arrived they *named* her Gladys but she was *called* Billie. Her full name was Gladys Iva Beaumont Howell. Billie was pretty, fair-haired, cute and charming; she had a sense of humour and a love of dance and drama. Gladys Havers, grandmother's eldest sister, after whom Billie was named, took a close interest in her and drew and painted many water-colour sketches of her.

Dulcie and Billie in
1911

Three sketches of Billie by Gladys Denham (formerly Havers, née Smedley)

The story was told that for many years her parents celebrated Billie's birthday on the 28th saying that, had she been born a year earlier, she might have been a leap-day child and have a birthday only once every four years. It was only when they needed to get a copy of her birth certificate that they realised their mistake.

The third child was born in September 1911 in Hankow[1] in northern China as hostilities built up in the Chinese rebellion.[2] 'She should be called Rebella.' suggested one aunt, 'Born in a rebellion and with a definite will of her own. Defiantly a girl when you really should have had a boy this time!' Not wishing to tempt fate, my grandparents ignored the advice and named her Elsie Marguerite - Elsie after her father's sister (who was generally known as 'Nainie') and Marguerite from her mother's middle name. Her great-grandmother Smedley had been Margaret but originated in Dundee in Scotland and it may be that she too was known as Marguerite.

The baby was entrusted to the care of an Amah.

---

[1] See www.willysthomas.net/OldChinaHankow :

Hankow, now known as Wuhan, was one of the Yangtze River cities opened up to foreign trade by the 1858 Treaty of Tientsin. Many famous clippers, such as the British Cutty Sark loaded tea at Hankow in the late 1860's and early 1870's.

The American travel writer Harry A. Franck wrote in the 1920's: *Hankow "is a bustling city, wholly Western in its architecture and layout, even though completely surrounded by China, its buildings looming high into the air, with several theaters, even though they offered only American movies, with automobiles dashing their imperious way up and down the river-front Bund."*

[2] In October of 1911, a group of revolutionaries in southern China led a successful revolt against the Qing Dynasty, establishing in its place the Republic of China and ending the imperial system.

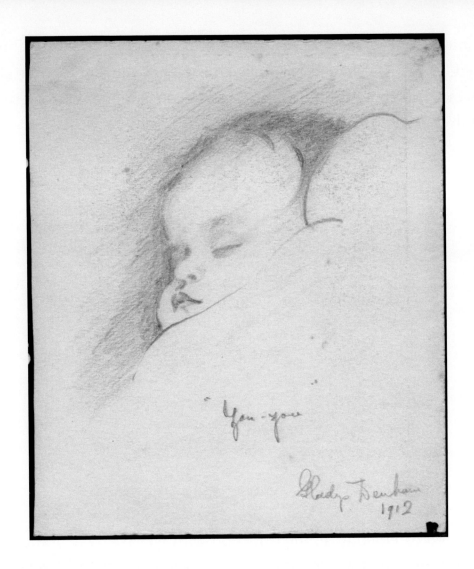

"You-you

Gladys Denham
1912

Amah had black hair, combed straight back in a tight bun. She wore a blue Chinese jacket and black trousers. She cradled little Elsie and watched over her as she slept.
'Zou Zou, Zou Zou!' said Amah. 'When she sleep she coo like the wood pigeon - Zou Zou, my little wood pigeon!'

Amah's nickname for the little girl stuck and throughout her young childhood the name Elsie was seldom used.   Later she was always Zou to her friends and family and only Elsie at school or otherwise officially.

In later years Gwen would often write to her daughter:

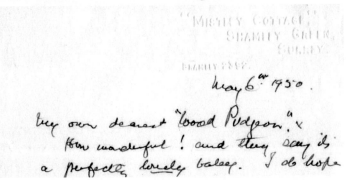

Zou said that 'Rebella' may not have been such a bad choice. As a child she often found she was the odd one out. While Dulcie and Billie played together she would often play imaginatively on her own. She could be outspoken and unconventional with a strong sense of justice and a dislike of any pretentiousness.

Zou Zou aged 3 by her aunt Gladys Denham

The name, Zou Zou, seemed to embody all the affection with which it was first coined and all the warmth her friends and family felt for her. She was as special and individual as her name.

My Zou Zou had at least two different Amahs. She was particularly fond of "Old Amah" who was a plump Chinese woman with a soft voice; she was filled with a tender love of children. Her name was Asam. She looked after the children in Chinkiang and was a simple soul. She had charge of the children when the adults went out in the evening, and she looked after them most of the day too until they were old enough for school. She would take them for walks and to see their friends and to Sunday School where they would sing 'Onward Christian Soldiers'. She washed their clothes and laid fresh, clean clothes out each morning and each afternoon. She entertained Zou Zou once by drawing a chicken for her. Zou Zou laughed to see that the misshapen bird had been given four legs. Amah was insistent and seemed offended that her drawing had been greeted with such derision.

Amah was perhaps the closest contact that my mother had with the Chinese. The colonial English did not usually mix socially with the local people. Grandfather had business with the rich Chinese merchants but as a rule the British, Europeans and

Americans kept apart from the Chinese. Grandfather knew a few Chinese words but most of the communication was in a Pidgin English.

Amah with Zou Zou and Old Amah with Willie

The Europeans all had Chinese servants - most houses would have a 'boy', a cook, a coolie for the odd jobs like cleaning the floors and lighting the fires, and (if there were children) an Amah. 'Boy' was the main house servant – the butler; it was he who dealt with the family and who in many households employed and controlled all the other servants. The children were forbidden to go into the kitchen - this was Cook's domain. He would take it as a personal affront should a member of the family appear to be checking up on how he ran his kitchen. Possibly he would take a proportion of the food for his own family or sell it on to other poor Chinese but a blind eye was turned to such practices. After all, if your household had a good cook and a faithful Boy then you could rely on them utterly to run a happy and efficient house.

So it was that the children saw very little of the true Chinese culture, and what they did see was hard for them to understand. My mother remembered the day Old Amah took off her black satin slippers to show her her feet. She had tiny feet.

'When a girl baby is born,' said Old Amah, 'it is not good. Boys are sons, girls are slaves! Girl, slave - it is the same word! If a family wants to marry their children well, the girls must be hard-working but also pretty - no huge feet like you English!' Amah started to unwind the Chinese silk bandages which she used as stockings.

'Like all girls at that time, when I was born my feet were tightly bound in silk to keep them small.'

My mother gasped to see them. Old Amah's feet were indeed small. Beside her big toe there were no other toes, but against the end of each foot, folded under it were little flat toes like pressed flowers - two-dimensional, delicate, butterfly wings!

'Oh, Amah! Didn't it hurt you? How could they do such a thing!'

'No, no, Zou Zou, I remember I used to cry with the pain but it went away! They did it so that I too could be beautiful and lucky and happy someday. They did their best for me.' And she smiled, that immaculate smile of bright white teeth and, as she slowly rebound her feet my mother realised that although old, Amah was indeed beautiful in a deep and lasting way.

The house in Amoy and, right, the girls with their father in the garden there in about 1914

Zou always loved animals and was particularly fond of birds later on. She said that all the time in China she took the native birds for granted and wished she had noticed them and drawn them.

Zou Zou's earliest memories dated back to when she was around two years old. She remembered feeling very ill and being put to bed: "It was lovely to lie down and shut my eyes because when I opened them, the wall I was facing seemed to move very close to me and the next moment it was far away."

She remembered being wrapped in a blanket and cuddled in her father's arms and being carried down from a boat to a waiting rickshaw. Gazing across a harbour she could see the city shrouded by the evening light and the lamps of the junks and the other ships reflected in the water. Her father remembered the occasion too.

'You were so ill!' he said. 'You had only just learnt to walk and then you got diphtheria. They put on a special carriage for us on the train to Shanghai. We all thought you would die. It was months before you were really well again.'

Zou Zou, Dulcie and Billie about 1913

The weakness meant she had to learn to walk a second time - she remembered the effort it took, hanging on to tables and chairs. The medicine had a different effect – Zou Zou's teeth turned a yellowish-brown. It made her all the more aware of Amah's lovely teeth - kept fine and white by regular salt washing and simple food. She became envious of her pretty sisters and always hid her smile behind her hand until her milk-teeth were replaced.

She also had scarlet fever not long after the diphtheria but came through both with the ministering of her mother and Old Amah.

Of course, Zou didn't remember much of the very early years. Her mother said that on the Siberian railway there was one stop where they all got out 'to stretch our legs' and she had heard a gasp of horror and turned to see her two-year-old with her arms around the neck of a large dog tied to some railings. It was a fierce sheepdog used to guard sheep and cattle from the wolves. These dogs were notoriously vicious and had had their tails and ears removed to make them less vulnerable to attack. But it took the child's affections calmly.

When war was declared in July 1914 they were in Chinkiang and she remembered going with her father to the Club and he walked so fast she had to run to keep up.

She remembered going to tea with Dr Bradshaw, whom she didn't like, but she was transfixed by his wife's beautiful red hair and by her singing. When she heard that Mrs Bradshaw had died she was sad because she wouldn't see that hair or hear her voice again.

Zou-Zou. Howell.

One New Year's Day in Chinkiang when my mother was four years old, the girls were called hurriedly in by their aunt: 'Wash your hands, tidy yourselves up and then go to your mother's room. She has a wonderful surprise for you.' Zou Zou wondered what it might be - a dress, a toy, a lovely new doll with pretty dresses and long hair to brush. That was what she really wanted most. By the time they got to the room she had convinced herself that that could be the only thing that could arouse such excitement in everyone! Her mother was in bed and Dulcie reached her first. 'Oh, how lovely!' said Dulcie. 'Ooo!' said Billie, smiling. Amah was bathing an ugly, bald baby. Zou Zou looked and a wrinkled, blotchy, red face sputtered back at her.

'Your new brother!' said her mother.

Tears sprang to Zou Zou's eyes at the awful disappointment! 'Oh, no!' she said, and fled from the room.

Old Amah;

Dulcie, Zou Zou and Billie with toddler Willie - 23rd April 1917;

Dulcie, Billie, Zou Zou and Willie c. 1921

Zou Zou aged 9

The family moved around from place to place seldom staying in one area for more than two years – from Hangkow to Chefoo, Amoy, Chinkiang, Chefoo again, Kobe, Hong Kong and visits to Yokahama, Shanghai and Peking. Various members of the family lived in the Far East and they were always welcomed to new towns by people they knew. Business was thriving and life was rich and carefree.

Zou Zou always loved drawing. A little story book, just 10 x 6 cm, made out of thin paper sewn together remains from her early childhood. It shows an understanding of perspective and attention to detail:

"The Story About Chingchong

One day Chingchong went for a walk when a lion sprang at him and he ran and climbed up a tree And some more man shot it and he went home."

In Chinkiang on Sundays Old Amah would take the children to Sunday School and they would sing 'Onward Christian Soldiers' and 'Jesus loves me'. There was no church there but missionaries ran the school and Sunday school. There were no shops only a market full of stalls and the children did not go there because it was crowded with Chinese and many beggars. Life in Chinkiang included picnics and social events at The Club and children's parties on St George's Day:

Dulcie   Billie   Zou Zou

Billie Dulcie Zou Zou & Willie

The four Howell children joined in the social life that revolved around the Club in Chinkiang.

There was always a similar centre for the foreigners who traded in the concessions in the various Chinese towns where they lived.

In 1918 the family moved from Chinkiang to a house in Chefoo.

The house at Chefoo

As children and young ladies (and there was no such thing as a teenager in those days) the three Howell sisters were encouraged in the arts. Their mother was an accomplished pianist and also wrote music for the plays that she and Lionel took part in. Aunt Gladys was a water-colourist, following her father in her love of art, and produced numerous paintings that still adorn the walls of the descendants of the family. Mother loved the piano and pleaded for music lessons but her skill in drawing meant that she was discouraged from music and encouraged to paint.

While Zou Zou was at school in Chefoo, she met a 'White Russian' girl called Helena Oustragraf who became her friend. Her family had fled there from Russia in 1917 but what became of them after the Howells moved on to Japan, Mother didn't know.

Zou is in the second row from top, next to a boy on the far right:

Chefoo School c.1919

Zou Zou, Helena Oustragraf, Billie, Dulcie and Vera Oustragraf

Zou remembered that once they had all been told to write a letter as an exercise. She chose to write to her grandmother, Laura Howell, in England. They had been taught a little about punctuation. The teacher had told them that a comma is used where there would be a natural break for a breath in a sentence. She was therefore astonished to see that little Elsie had put a comma after every word. When challenged she said: "My grandmother is very old and she will probably need to breathe very often."

In 1921 the family visited England. The trip may have been to visit Lionel's mother in Westcliff-on-Sea and also to deliver Billie to school in Lincolnshire for the first time. Willie and his parents stayed in a Southend boarding house over the summer. Laura Howell's house at 39 West Road was full. She had two of her grandchildren, Ian and Mollie Howell, living with her and also Charlotte (Lottie) Martin aged 22. Lottie was the daughter of a sea captain who had worked for Butterfield and Swire. Lottie had been sent back to England to attend Laura's sisters' school and lived with Laura, by then a widow, as an adopted daughter.

Trudy, Edith and Kate Harrington at their school;   *Lance Howell and Lottie 1905;*   *Lottie and Zou Zou 1923.*

Zou Zou was nine at the time so she also stayed with Dulcie and Billie at their school for the summer term - the youngest girl there. She appears on the 1921 census at Hartington House School in Woodhall Spa.

On their return the family moved to Japan via Hong Kong.

"Mother, Dad, Willie and I arrived back after six months leave in England, leaving Dulcie and Billie at boarding school in Woodhall Spa. Hong

Kong was a dull, built-up place. When our family were away in England, Old Amah would go to stay with her daughter in Canton but she always met us at the wharf when we returned to China. We stayed at the Peak Hotel and I went to school. We only had six months in Hong Kong and then we were sent to Kobe in Japan.

Edward, the Prince of Wales was visiting Hong Kong in HMS Renown and we went aboard with a crowd of people to be shown over it. When we got to Kobe the Renown was there too and we school children with everyone else paraded and waved flags and Prince Edward was introduced to the head teacher. I was not very impressed.

Kobe was a nice town we stayed at the Tor Hotel until my father found a house for us. The hotel had a lovely Japanese garden with stone lamps in which a candle burned at night and of course a beautiful bridge across a pool with goldfish and water lilies and lovely shrubs and trees. The manager's wife often sat near one of the pools and did needlework while her son played. She was always shouting at the poor child something that sounded like a string of names: "Henrietta Joséa Wasser[3], don't do that." and "Henrietta Joséa Wasser, come here." One day I found him catching tadpoles and skinning them and then throwing them back in the pond. I was very angry and said he was not to do that. He took no notice so I said "I hope you fall in and get a mouthful." Shortly afterwards he did just that and 'Mrs Wasser' pulled him out and he was coughing up tadpoles.

After being at the hotel some time my father rented a house and we moved in. It was quite a nice house except for one thing – no one liked to use the dining room except for meals. One night I could not get to sleep and as I lay on my bed I heard someone come out of the dining room and come upstairs and then along the passage to the room opposite my

---

[3] The manager or the Tor Hotel was Alfred Mildner, a German from Alsace Lorraine, so it might have been some German phrase warning Henry about going too close to the water.

bedroom. I called out thinking it was Old Amah but got no answer. After hearing this I decided to get up and see who it was. So when I heard it next time I got up and stood at my bedroom door. The passage light was on and I counted each step on the stairs I found there was no one there. I told my mother and she said it was nothing and changed the subject. However, when my father had to go to on business my mother used to have my brother or myself sleep with her. Then one of my nights as I lay in bed I heard the footsteps begin. To my surprise my mother got out of bed, grabbed my hand and said "Come on" We went to her bedroom door; the passage light was on and we both stood and counted each step. When the footsteps came to the top there was no one there.

When my father came back he started looking for another house. One he looked at was just at the bottom of our small garden. When the evenings closed in I saw a Japanese woman carrying a candle. She had a small altar and I could see she burned joss sticks and said her prayers. She was the caretaker and took my father all over the house. He noticed a door in the hall and asked what was there, she said the cellar and he said he would like to see it. She didn't seem to want to show him and said it was very dark but in the end she took my father down and to his horror he saw a leper in the last stages of that dreadful disease. I don't know what happened after that but we certainly did not take that house.

My father found a beautiful house in Kobe. As we could not move into the house for another six months we rented a lovely house in Shioya with a beautiful pond running the whole length of the gardens and a bridge across it. It overlooked the beach below and the sea. Our Japanese landlord lived next door and between us was a boat house through which we used to go down to the beach. Behind the boat house, dividing our house from his, was a greenhouse full of orchids. I loved Shioya and William and I used to play on the beach all day. I don't think we wore shoes the whole time just Japanese sandals or 'geta'. After tea we used to walk quite a way up the beach to watch the Japanese pull up their

18

fishing nets. They sorted out the fish to sell and ones they couldn't use were chucked back into the sea. William and I used to walk slowly home throwing stranded fish back into deep water. Once when I watched them being brought in, the fishermen were very upset as they had caught a turtle in the net and it had died as it couldn't get the surface for air. Turtles are sacred to the Japanese so they buried it in the sand and made a mound on top and stuck paper flowers all over it. Three days later some monks from a temple in the hills behind us came down carrying a black lacquer coffin with a gold design on it placed the turtle in it and took it back to their temple to be buried. At the same time as this a Japanese man had committed suicide by flinging himself in front of a train just by our front gate and was left there for about five days."

In Kobe their house was large and white and overlooked the sea:

"The house had a marble staircase with wrought iron banisters and lovely big rooms. The sitting room had sliding doors into the dining room and a door through the other side into a music room and at the end of the hall was a study. In the flower garden there were three large pine trees and under them was an altar to burn joss sticks where Japanese would come to say prayers. The story was that three very holy pilgrims died in that spot and the three trees grew from the places they died. One of the trees was leaning over badly - I am told they later had to take it down."

The Howell family house in Kobe.

Zou Zou's sisters had tended to play together and they both started school before her. Her brother was too young and insensitive and so it was that she was often left to her own devices - happily dreaming, playing, drawing, observing the world around her with delight and imagination. She would find little caves in the rocks or among the roots of trees and decorate them with tiny furniture and flowers to make comfortable homes for the fairy folk. One day while completing a fairy bower she saw a slight movement. She froze - there about ten feet from her, was a tiny, perfect little person. It was no more than fifteen inches tall and was dressed in green. The fairy was looking at the little girl's fairy houses. After a moment it seemed to realise it had been seen because it scuttled away and disappeared into the foliage. Now, you may well think this is not a true story, but like most of the others within this collection, my mother told it to me and she swore it was true. I have no reason to doubt it.

The beach near the house was full of wonders. The clear bluish water was warm and lapped gently on the beach. If you waded in, little fish would swirl around you and sometimes bump into your legs. At certain times of year the Japanese would come at dusk to the beach and launch little paper boats with offerings to the ancestral spirits. Each boat held a lighted candle and would be driven out to sea as the shore breezes caught in its paper sail. The following morning Zou Zou and little William would comb the beach for the wrecks and sometimes they found a perfect boat in which the candle had been snuffed out by the wind or water. These boats were beautiful, carefully made things, too fragile for children's toys.

"In Japan I just ran wild. It was beautiful there. I usually went barefoot except when I went to school," said my mother. "We were sent to Mrs Davidge's school and after all that freedom I hated it!" The school catered for all the European and American young children. "Mrs Davidge would rap your knuckles with a ruler if you got your arithmetic wrong." That put my mother off maths for ever. She always claimed to hate it but later was able to deal with her own finances perfectly adequately.

The one joy that came from that school was that my mother made new friends. A young American girl called Mary Sjobek (left) became as close as a sister to her. Mary went back to America after three years and they wrote regularly to each other until their next meeting over forty years later. Many of my mother's letters were returned to me after Mary's death. Unfortunately I have hardly any of Mary's letters to her. They were frequent and the writing became well known to me.

Lionel's sister Elsie ('Nainie') with her husband Colin Ford

and Zou Zou's cousins

Edith, Barbara, Audrey and Colin

As well as friends, the children had a number of cousins in the Far East. There were Ian and Mollie Howell, the children of Lionel's brother, William and his first wife Belle. Lionel's sister, Nainie, married Colin Ford and had four children, Barbara, Audrey, Colin and Edith. Gwen's sister, Iva, married twice and had five sons and a daughter: Hugh Smith and Freddie, Pat, Bobby, Piers and Daphne Rickard. Another of her sisters, Dulcie, had a girl, Noelle, and a boy, Dick Danby.

Noelle Danby was known by her nickname 'Pixie'.

Zou Zou, Dulcie, Pixie and Billie in Chinkiang and Pixie later in Peking.

21

Sadly, Pixie got scarlet fever and became very ill as she and her family were travelling to England via the Trans-Siberian Railway. She died on the train aged about twelve.

Family and friends all moved often and sometimes they would not see each other for some time. The Rickards moved to England and settled in Bedford where for a time Fred Rickard was the mayor. There they were able to host the Howell children sometimes once they were sent to school in England.

Travelling to the local school wherever they were in China or Japan either meant a short walk or a rickshaw ride. The rickshaw was a chair with wheels and it was pulled at a good rate by a coolie. Zou Zou found it fascinating to watch the rhythmic tread of his bare feet as the man pulled his rickshaw. When it was wet, the mud would ooze up between his toes.

"My memories of China and Japan are vivid and mostly happy. The Far East can be very beautiful. The buildings are delicate and made from finely carved stone and wood lacquered with deep red or black. Porcelain dragons and birds are the corner tiles on the roofs. China is a land of delicacy but also of great cruelty."

"Chinkiang was a horrid place as I remember it. There were beggars everywhere. The only shops were stalls in a rough market and we weren't allowed to go there. We lived in a flat with a huge roof garden. It was over the 'go-downs'. They were the storehouses and were full of sugar – brown, white and candy sugar off the ships. We three girls went to an American Missionary school about two miles away. We were carried there in a cane chair borne by four coolies. On the way to school we always passed a lean-to hut made of bamboo matting. Lepers used to sit under it and beg – they would call out and spit at us as we went by. It used to frighten me"

In the countryside there were often shrines. It was said that peasants would go to pray for good luck and to give offerings so that they would have sons. In one place there was a well where newly-born unwanted daughters were often left to their fate. A woman bringing her own unwanted baby would push any infant there into the well and replace it with her own. That way she made an offering to the gods but did not kill her own child. Some Christian nuns built an orphanage nearby and used to save the poor babies.

Not all were lucky. One day, when Zou Zou was six, the Howell children went with their friends on a picnic. The weather was lovely, their spirits high and the scenery was beautiful and dramatic. Nearby where they stopped there were some Chinese burial mounds.

"The Chinese bury their dead anywhere and most graves are a large mound and on top the earth is pressed into a bucket shape like a child's sandcastle· We were thoughtless like most children and ran up the mounds and kicked the bucket shaped earth off the top."

The adults fussed with the picnic paraphernalia, laying out cloths and unpacking the baskets.

'Why don't you children see how many times you can run around that big mound before we are ready to eat?' said Mrs Paxton. The children were delighted by the idea and ran to the mound. It seemed to have been cut out of the hill and the cutting made a kind of dry moat around it. So round the moat they ran, but Dulcie stopped: 'There's a pile of clothes up there.' She and a boy scrambled up the embankment. Her expression changed, 'No! Don't come up, don't look!' she said as they hurried back down, but it was too late. There was a neat pile of new, carefully folded clothes; a child's clothes. Behind the pile was the body of a Chinese child of about three. She had been cut in half and only the upper part of the body was there.

"We had our picnic lunch and then went home!" said my mother as she told me the story. *"We were all shaken and I was crying· When we got home, my father tried to cheer us up by playing and singing at the piano· I remember he played 'Polly-Wolly-Doodle' and lots of other cheerful songs· However the last song was an unfortunate choice: 'Wrap me up in my Tarpaulin Jacket' and I fled from the room in tears· I can still see that child as clearly as if it were yesterday, and I hate that song."*

Dulcie, Lionel, Zou Zou, Gwen and Billie

Willie, Gladys and Billie

A miniature of Billie and Dulcie from a photograph taken about 1911,

by Zou Zou in 1934.

Zou Zou's Story: 'Back Home'

In Kobe and in China the small children had quite a high degree of freedom. The time came when she was twelve to send her "Home" to a proper school where she would be taught all that a young lady in the 1920s would need to know. Going "Home" was a strange thing because it was very unlike *home*. She recalled that while travelling in England for the first time, she saw a woman scrubbing her own front doorstep; why didn't the coolie do it?

Zou Zou's aunts, Dulcie Danby and Iva Rickard, both spent some time in England. Iva had returned with her husband, Fred Rickard, to live in Bedford. All their boys went to Bedford School (as did Willie Howell and Dick Danby). Fred became mayor of Bedford and a pillar of society there.

Lionel's aunts, Trudie and Edith Harrington, ran Lancefield School for Girls in Southend and his nieces Barbara and Audrey Ford went there. However, that school was probably closed by the time Edith Ford and the Howell girls grew old enough, so a school in Lincolnshire was chosen for them.

So it was that Dulcie was already at Miss Lunn's School for Girls at Hartington House in Woodhall Spa when Billie (12) and Zou Zou (9) visited her in 1921 in time to be recorded on the census that year. Their parents and Willie spent the term time with Lionel's mother in Westcliffe. Billie was now old enough to remain at the school but after Christmas Zou Zou, her brother and parents returned to Japan by ship via China. Zou Zou would start at Hartington House once she too was about 12.

*Zou Zou,
cousin Edith Ford,
another girl and Billie
in 1921 on the first visit to
Woodhall Spa.*

The girls at Woodhall Spa showing Dulcie, Billie and their cousin Edith

Lionel wrote to Dulcie and Billie at school as the family returned to Japan in 1921.

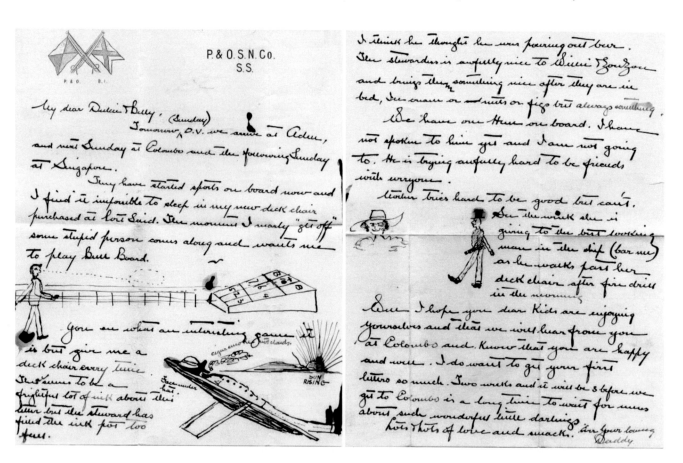

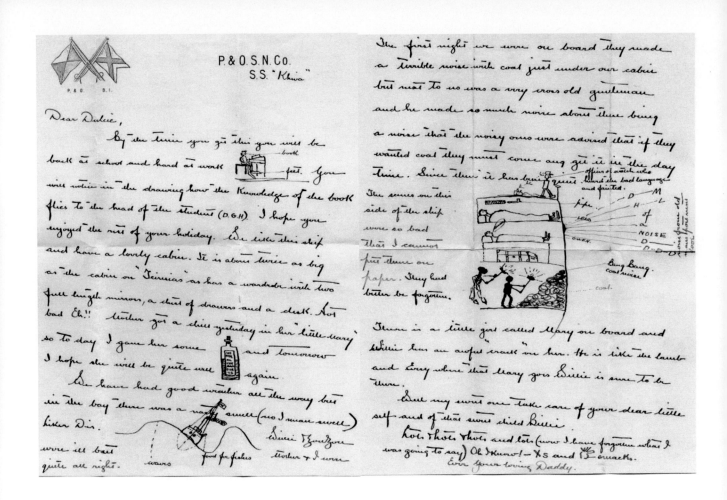

Zou Zou wrote happily to her sisters and, like her father, she included drawings to amuse them. She always complained that she got badly sea-sick and would feel ill in anticipation of any trip by boat.

It isent a sunday it a rainday

June 10TH
Sunday

Dear Dulcie and Billie

We have finished THE SON OF TARZAN and we havent any more to read so will you please send the next book. Tony is quite big. Do you know I might go to England in the Autumn. Their is a new girl coming to your school from Kobe I know her, her name is Roscie, she has short hair and it is curlie. Give Miriam Hall my love and Edith too Amah sends her love and her chin chin. Dosent Willie write nicely for 7. I give Willie school. I made this tofry up about pussy it is true. Is cause my dad writing and pug mess sent it ofale.

Do you know if you give pussy a bone she will eate the bone and, all but not you.

The other day we saw a sea plane on the water. To day mr Seton — Winton went away to Shanghi, his wife is dead she I knew her she was afly nice.

I have a little pussy the sweetest ever seen her coat is black and white and so so neat and clean.

A cat came up and bit her and bit her on the toe and know she limps along were ever she dose

It is quite 8.30 so good by till to morrow

XXXXXXXX

from you.

MERRY XMAS To you

On 1st September 1923 at noon, while the family was eating together in the house at Kobe, her mother looked up to see the ceiling light swinging to and fro. "Oh no!" she said. "An earthquake!"

It was indeed a devastating earthquake with the epicentre near Yokohama and Tokyo. The collapsing buildings, and fires and tsunami that resulted killed many people. Refugees were brought to Kobe and the family housed a man. Lionel wrote to Billie and Dulcie:

"*Yokohama was just wiped out in about 10 seconds and what was left was burnt afterwards. Tokio did not get it so badly but the fires there afterwards were bad. In one place about 40,000 people got cornered and all were burnt. The losses in Tokio were probably about 80,000 people but in Yokohama about 180,000. Then you have to consider all the losses for 100 miles each way. You have no idea what a terrible calamity it has been.*

It was awfully sad to see the poor refugees arrive, some without wives others without husbands or children; hardly anything on and not a thing left in the world. One girl was awfully proud because she had a bathing suit on but it was pinned all the way to keep it together. Mrs Harley arrived in Kobe with a kimono lent her by one of the officers and a sun hat lent by another. They had jumped from burning lighter to burning lighter and had to throw water over each other to prevent their clothes from burning. Another of our men was in the water 5 hours hanging onto a bit of wood because he could not swim. He had to duck every now and

then the heat was so great. When he was picked up he was quite blind.
His sight has returned but the poor chap's nerves are all to pieces."

My mother told me that this man later died from all the oily water he had ingested.

"Today there is an advertisement in the paper "Found on Yokohama
Bluff a little boy, blond, blue eyes, one year old. Can anyone claim him or
give information?" Poor little chap, probably both his parents are killed
and he may never know what his name is. That's only one case but there
are many like that. I have telegrams in the office asking for news of
several but they will never be found and their fate will never be known.

We have a man living with us whose house fell over the Bluff, 150
feet, with him in it. He arrived at the bottom with a piano one side of
him and a wardrobe the other and his dog at his feet. Master and dog
got up unhurt and went to look for the mistress, his wife. She was also
unhurt although she had been buried under the house, part of which had
remained on top.

There were some wonderful escapes which one likes to hear about, but
there are some terrible tales which I cannot tell you because they would
make your little hairs stand on end."

Gwen wrote to them with similar news. She said gas and water pipes were broken, the
ships in the harbour were thrown together and damaged; lighthouses bent and cracked,
the breakwater lifted high in some places and disappeared in others. The water level at
the lake at Hakone (100 km from Tokyo)
"dropped 4 feet then they felt the earthquake and the hotel fell flat ".

Needless to say this catastrophe disrupted business and the family packed their
belongings and moved to Hong Kong two months later.

Zou knew she would miss Japan. Her father's letters to England reverted to their usual
illustrated, witty descriptions. His letter describing the move is light-hearted:

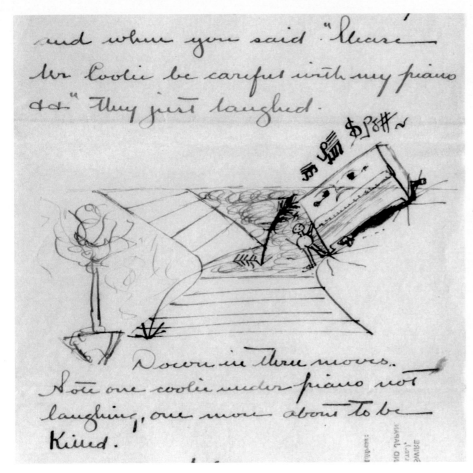

"... and when you said "Please Mr Coolie, be careful with my piano etc." they just laughed. Down in three moves.

Note one coolie under piano not laughing, one more about to be killed."

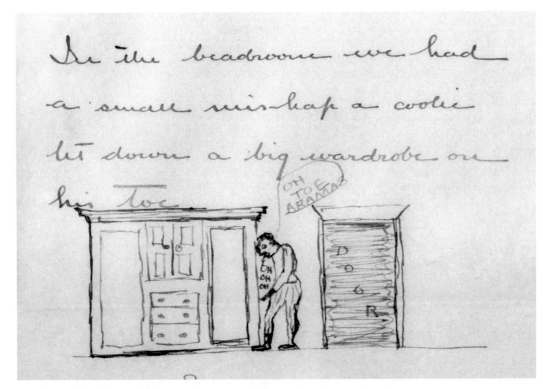

"In the bedroom we had a small mishap – a coolie let down a big wardrobe on his toe."

"This is Father – carrying a picture or doing light work.

Mother brings the family jewels. (light work)
JEW –
"ELERY" are on the other side of the box and cannot be seen.

Willie brings the clothes basket, also light work.

Zou Zou, also fond of light work, brings a toothbrush.
This is how she feels while carrying it. "

"Mother, Willie and Zou Zou arrived by car with the animals.
Chorus: "Toot Toot, Meow meow, Bow wow, Twit twit, Pip pip, Chirp chirp "Not a cent, not a cent" (Willie), "Lovie Duckie, Lovie Duckie" (Zou Zou)
"Hi er Koo. Hi er koo" (Mother)
Japanese for be quick.
"Hi Hi" (chauffeur)
Japanese for Yes, Madam"

*Old
Amah
and her
luggage*

The following May (1924) Zou Zou came to England in order to join her sisters at school. She travelled with her Aunt Nainie Ford, her cousin Barbara and Barbara's husband Keith Watson. They took a ship to Marseilles and then the sleeper train to Paris and on to Calais from where they took the ferry. Finally they arrived in Westcliffe, Southend at her grandmother's house and then Colin and Edith Ford arrived to greet them. She wrote to her sisters when she arrived in England. Zou's letter to her sisters shows her excitement and interest in the places and sights. They had been in contact with measles and smallpox on their travels. Zou thought she might have to quarantine before going to the school.

Laura Howell, Zou Zou's grandmother, was 69 in 1924 and probably seemed quite old. Zou recollected that when the girls were in the house they were largely ignored and Laura would put on headphones and listen to the radio through her "crystal set".

The school in Lincolnshire was run by Headmistress Miss "Sally" (Susanna) Lunn with help from her sister Catherine as housekeeper and several servants and a matron. One of Billie's photos shows "Florence Lunn" – possibly another sister or the alternative name for Catherine. The Lunn spinsters had a famous brother in Dr Henry S. Lunn (1859 – 1939) – a medical missionary who founded the H. S. Lunn Travel Company, later Lunn Poly.

Zou Zou didn't really enjoy school. Her somewhat haphazard education so far had not prepared her for boarding school. She felt homesick and she was a bit shy. She recalled it as a small school with maybe fifty or sixty pupils at most. But there was one teacher who was able to make her feel more at home and that was Miss Joachim who became the head.

Sally Lunn　　*Florence Lunn*　*Miss Joachim*　　*Misses Joachim, Parr and Savage*

At school in the afternoon after lessons, the girls used to sit around the fire and do sewing and write letters and have a cup of tea under a teacher's watchful eye. On one of these occasions during Zou Zou's first term, the teacher said to her: "Elsie, go into the kitchen and see whether the kettle is boiling." Dutifully she went into the kitchen where a large kettle was hissing on the stove but she felt a sense of panic. In China she had never entered the kitchen; it was forbidden. You could lose a good servant in this way. So Zou Zou had never seen a kettle boil. She returned to the drawing room.
"How can I tell whether it is boiling?" she asked, to the surprise of the other girls.

The School Certificate Examination (often called the "Junior Certificate") was usually taken at age 16. Students had to gain six passes, including English and Mathematics, to obtain a certificate or they could obtain a "matriculation exemption" with a credit in five subjects, including English, Mathematics, Science and a language. It seems that Dulcie got her certificate in 1923 and Billie passed in 1924. Dulcie was Head Girl when Zou arrived but shortly after Zou Zou started at the school Dulcie left. That October she travelled home to China on the SS "Teiresias", a Blue Funnel Line ship, from Liverpool with her aunt Nainie Ford and Edith.

Girls outside; and below: the Dormitory

Dulcie and Billie;

Girl Guides: Zou Zou is first in the bottom row

There was a Girl Guide troop at Woodhall Spa School but all they seemed to do was march and drill and it didn't interest Zou Zou. For sports they played hockey, lacrosse and tennis.

Billie took photographs of girls dancing and doing Classical Greek poses.

The school also put on plays and concerts and Billie loved acting and dancing.

Billie took part in all the dramatic events and it may have been this that made her such a favourite at the school that she was made Head Girl. Later she went to R.A.D.A. where a fellow student was John Boxer (who appeared in "Ghandi" and "Bridge over the River Quai").

Zou Zou couldn't act. In fact she couldn't imitate accents and her voice and accent remained set. She spoke quietly with an accent which sometimes betrayed her colonial past. There were some words that she pronounced wrongly or as they had in China and her spelling was odd. She was intelligent but her education had been mixed. She told me that she knew her accent sometimes made her seem different and she always felt slightly foreign because her childhood home had not been in England. She was eager to leave school. However, she had to take her matriculation exams and then to retake them because of her low maths score.

Zou Zou's talents were in art. She had inherited her grandfather's eye for detail and it hadn't gone un-noticed. *"My writing"* she said, *"was not very special, but one year they asked me to produce the programmes for the school play. I did them all by hand, carefully writing them out in a flowery script to make them look beautiful. After that my writing was different!"* Many years later it was her distinctive writing that reunited her with one of her art-school friends, Mollie Cockram; Mollie's husband Henry Martin, a lawyer, saw a letter on another man's desk and, recognising the writing, took her address so that Mollie could write to her.

In the school holidays it was too far to return to China so the girls had to be found places to stay in England. At these times they were sometimes able to stay with family and met their cousins. Zou Zou recalled playing "sardines" one Christmas with cousins and friends. The game meant several people hid and the others searched and hid with whoever they found until all were hiding. Zou found Colin Ford and hid in a cupboard with him. There he gave her her first kiss.

Often holidays were spent with strangers. For one summer they stayed in Kent at a farmhouse, Smallhythe Place, owned by Ellen Terry, a well-known actress who died aged 81 in 1928, only a year or so after the Howell girls had stayed there for the last time. The house is now a National Trust property. There was an orchard and fields. Zou Zou used to climb an orchard tree and hide in its branches to keep out of the way of visitors or chores while she read. She would sometimes eat the apples and learnt the hard way that unripe fruit can give you a bad tummy-ache.

The sisters usually were together in the holidays. Several times they stayed at a farm owned by Miss Apletree and Miss Collins where there were cattle and sheep in the fields. On one occasion Dulcie and Billie had been walking across a field together when they were charged by a bull; Dulcie scrambled up a tree and pulled Billie up just in time. They were stuck there until the bull went far enough away for them to make it to the gate. Dulcie recalled that she couldn't understand where she had found the strength to lift her sister so deftly; had there been no emergency she wouldn't have been able to do it.

Zou , Freddie, Pat and Willie

Some holidays were spent with Aunt Iva and Uncle Fred Rickard who were in Bedford for a time. They had a large family. Iva had married a man called Hugh Smith who had died. They had one son also called Hugh. The Rickards were Freddie, Pat, Bobby, Daphne and Piers. Mother had a soft spot for Freddie and was roughly the same age as Bobby and liked him but she found Pat "bumptious"; I think he may have teased her. At breakfast she remembers that the boys were allowed either butter or jam on their toast but Daphne was given both because she was a girl. Zou Zou therefore refused to take both, although entreated to do so, and had only the butter. Having lived in China where cows' milk was a rarity, she always loved full-cream milk and butter.

She remembered Piers, the youngest, as perhaps the cleverest and most intriguing of the Rickard boys; Piers could charm birds out of the hedges; when he went into a garden it seemed the butterflies would flock around him. He was fascinated by nature and science. At school his science teacher would tell him what exhibits he needed for the next biology lesson and Piers would bring them – amoebas, frogs, fungi, anything that might be found in the wild. Piers was destined for Cambridge to read Biology but the war intervened and he was killed aged 19 at Dunkirk.

She didn't keep contact with any of her school friends except for a girl called Mab Forshaw, whom she had once saved from a bully and who had adored her ever since. That girl would write regularly until during the war when the flow of letters suddenly stopped. Her last communication had a picture of her with her two children, Juliet and John (about 4 and 2 years old), in 1941

In 1926 Lionel stopped working for Butterfield and Swire. Lionel, Gwen and Willie returned to England for a few years and took a house at 25 Cole Park in Twickenham. What drew them back to England was probably that Laura, his mother, was ill and went into a care-home where she died in 1928.

The house in Twickenham

and Willie, Pat, Zou, Billie, Gwen and Lionel in the garden there.

Zou Zou couldn't wait to leave school and was pleased in 1928, at seventeen, when at last she could start Art School in London.

By 1933 her parents were back in Peking and Lionel was busy setting up his own business dealing in exports and imports of British goods and stocks and shares.

Zou in about 1928

Zou Zou's Story: Art College

Zou Zou's talents were in drawing and painting, talents initially inherited and learnt from the Smedley family. On leaving school she attended the Royal Academy School – where the teacher told her that she "drew like a man" implying that she should soften her style to suit her gender! Since most famous artists were men, she said she took it as a back-handed compliment. Contemporaries at art college with her were Peter Scott and also Mervyn Peake. However, she moved to St John's Wood Art College to complete her course.

St John's Wood Art School had originally been founded in 1878 to prepare students for study at the Royal Academy. In the 1930's this association was strengthened when the President of the Royal Academy, Sir William Llewellyn, became its Patron. However, by this time the St John's Wood School flourished as an institution independent of subsidy and free from outside jurisdiction and enjoyed the patronage of painters such as Sir George Clausen, Sir John Lavery, and Sir Alfred Munnings. There were Courses in Life Drawing and Painting, Head and Costume, Drawing and Painting from Still Life, Antique Drapery etc., Anatomy Observation and Memory, Lettering, Composition, Poster Painting Design, Architectural and Perspective drawing and Mural Decorations.

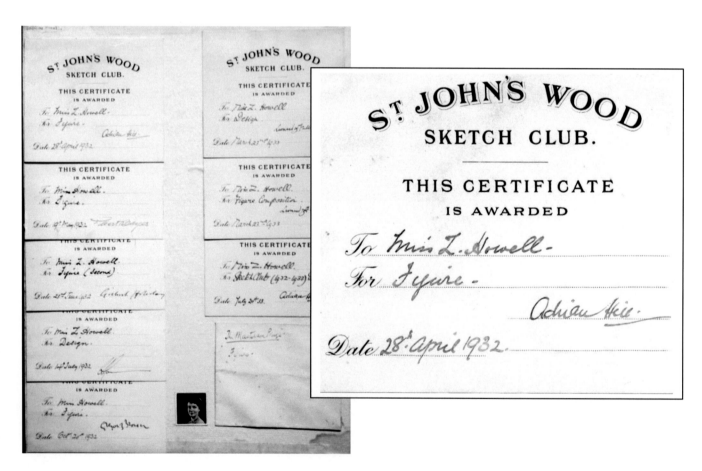

During the 1930s the School also organised The St John's Wood Sketch Club, presided over by Clausen. Four subjects were given each month to each member and the sketches were criticised by visiting artists and a certificate awarded for the best work in each division. At the end of the year prizes were awarded for the best work done during the year.[1]

Zou gained a number of certificates and the Masterson Prize for her figure drawing.

Some certificates are signed by Adrian Hill who was an alumnus of the school. He became famous in the 1950s for his children's television show where he drew pictures using charcoal and chalk and showed a gallery of entries sent in by his viewers.

Gervas

Ursula

Zou moved to a flat at 124 Cheyne Walk in Chelsea which she shared with another student called Ursula Cox. She was friends with Connie Pope and Mollie Cockram. They had other friends too – a young man called Sinclair and another called Gervas Taylor who had been at Bedford School and therefore knew Willie and the Rickard cousins.

She kept herself by working part time on the Tote at White City. Once, when she took me to London in the '50s, we saw a strangely-dressed man on Waterloo Station and she said he had been one of those who bet on the dogs when she was there.

---

[1] from www.stjohnswoodmemories.org.uk   st-johns-wood-art-school

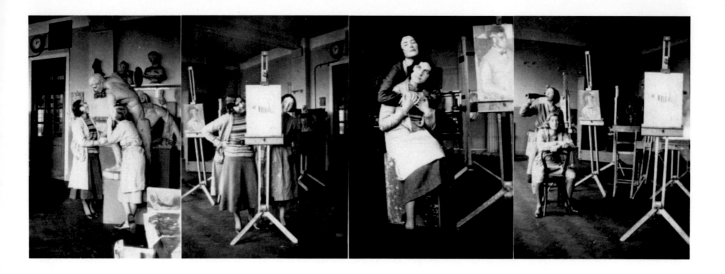

She told me that those were some of the best days of her life. She had a natural talent. They were taught perspective and shown how to work it out mathematically. In her exam she was given a description of a scene and was supposed to do the measuring to produce a picture of it. Ever since the rapped knuckles in Miss Davidge's school, she had considered herself hopeless at maths, so she read the description and from it drew the scene without any calculations at all. She got top marks for it.

Group of students – with Zou 3rd from right

A room at 124 Cheyne Walk

Gervas graduated from Cambridge and then trained as a teacher. The late 1920s and early '30s was a bad time for young men starting work. He got a job at a school but after a year, instead of giving him a raise in salary, they sacked him and appointed another newly-qualified teacher.   He was, however, a very positive character, always happy, intelligent and witty too. It was no surprise that Zou Zou and he became engaged.

Gervas, Willie and Zou on a punt at Cambridge.

Guida, Zou Zou, Mollie Cockram and Guy Thorpe in Folkestone

A large portfolio of Zou Zou's drawings has survived from her art-school days showing that she was a highly-skilled and sensitive artist and particularly skilled in portraiture.

Here are a few photos.

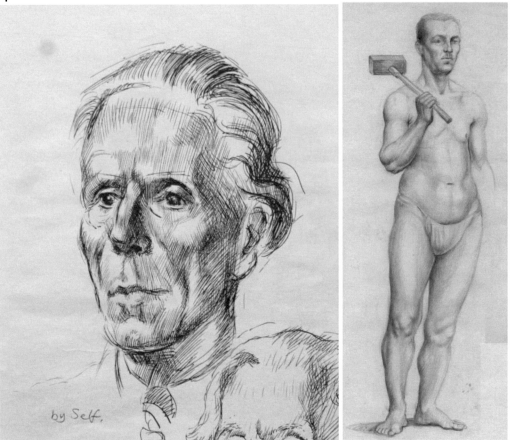

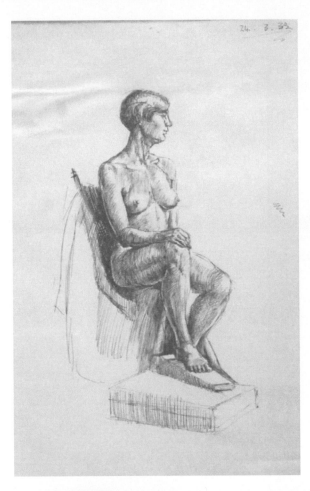

Circus Road Studio at St John's Wood

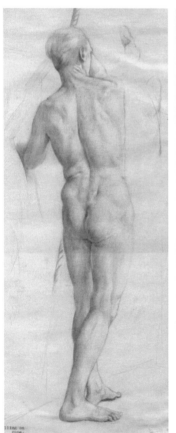

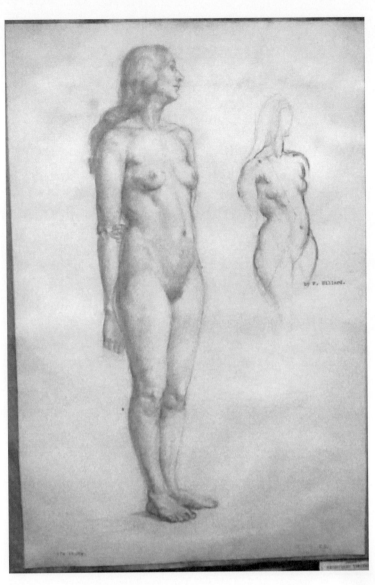

Drawings from life

Connie Pope (painted on fine tissue paper) and "My Feet"

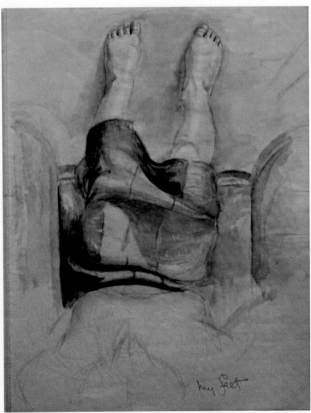

47

Quick sketch of Sitwell.

Pauline Sitwell

48

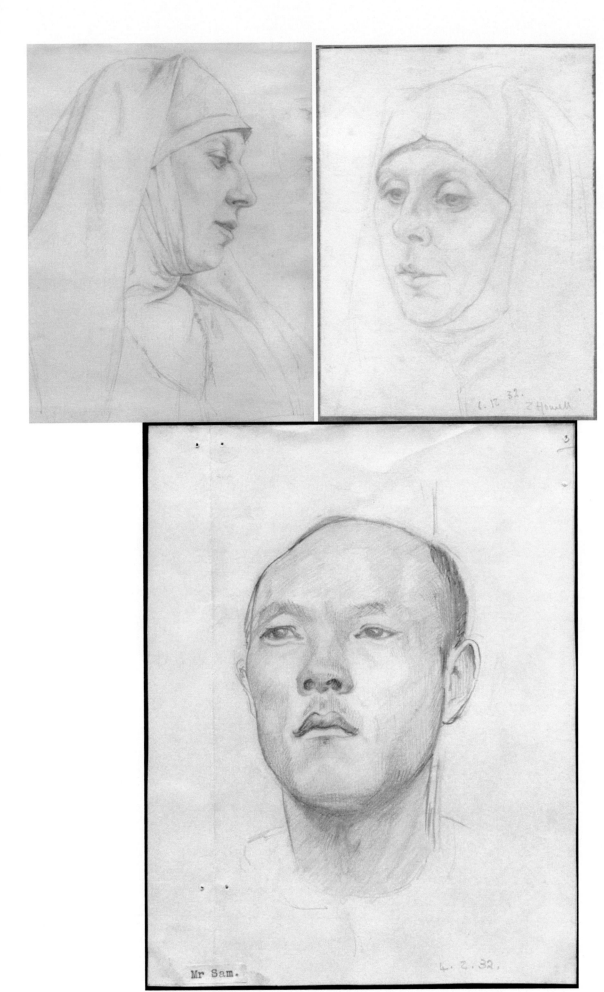

Mr Sam.

49

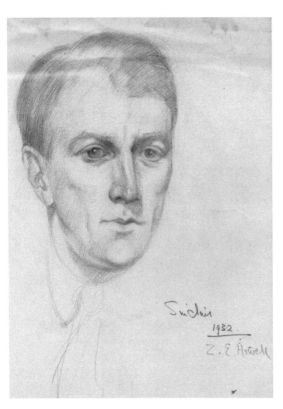

Sinclair was a friend of Gervas and Zou Zou in London.

BOARD OF EDUCATION

EXAMINATIONS IN ART

THIS IS TO CERTIFY THAT
IN THE YEAR 1933

Marguerite Howell

PASSED THE EXAMINATION
IN DRAWING

COMPRISING TESTS IN DRAWING
FROM THE ANTIQUE, DRAWING
FROM LIFE, DRAWING FROM
MEMORY AND KNOWLEDGE,
ANATOMY, PERSPECTIVE, AND
ARCHITECTURAL DRAWING.

1st AUGUST, 1933.   PRINCIPAL ASSISTANT SECRETARY.

On leaving art school Zou Zou applied for several jobs and was delighted to be offered a position in a new animation firm working on the films. She told me she would have earned £2 a week, which was a good wage in those days. She wrote to her mother and father to ask whether she should accept the job. Their reply was a ticket for the journey to take her back to Peking. She always regretted not taking that job and leaving Gervas in England. She expected to return soon. She told me that when she got back to her parents' home she was wearing the engagement ring:

"Mother never once asked to look at it. I think she had heard from her sister, Dulcie (Danby), that Gervas was only a teacher and was not from a particularly well-to-do family. Mrs Taylor, his mother, was so kind

51

and I really liked his sister, Frances· I often thought they would have been so much nicer as in-laws than the ones I ended up with!"

Willie and she returned to China together on the S.S. Conte Rosso in September 1933. Willie would have just left school.

After many months the possibility of her return to England faded and the engagement was sadly broken off.

Gervas, as a teacher, was not conscripted into the forces during the war but became a fire-fighter in London. He died doing this work in London during the blitz.

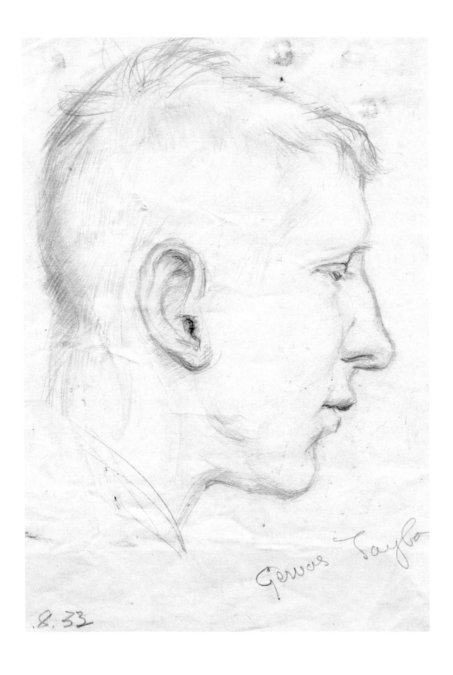

Zou Zou's Story: Peking in the 1930s

Life in Peking for a young Englishwoman was taken up with the social whirl of the expatriate British society: cocktail parties, races and events organized at the Club. The gentlemen had in addition their business which brought them into contact with Chinese.

Dulcie:

On leaving school at the age of seventeen (1924), Dulcie had returned to China and had married Geoffrey Ingham Larkins in Dairen on 23rd October 1926. They were unable to have children probably because of a near-fatal injury that Geoff had suffered at the Battle of Passchendaele. It was said that his batman pushed his intestines back into place and bound him up before the stretcher-bearers took him away; he was lucky to survive. Dulcie and Geoff were, however, very happy together for a very long time. Geoff had an older brother, Douglas. When Doug's wife died shortly after the birth of their son Peter, Dulcie and Geoff went to live with Doug and brought up the boy as their own.

Geoff and Dulcie's wedding; Peter and Dulcie; Doug and Mabel

A regular visitor was Mabel who was the sister of Doug's deceased wife. Doug and she decided to get married but this was not possible in some countries as it was considered as "marrying your sister". Eventually they did marry and they then moved to their own place and took Peter with them. Dulcie had to accept this. As far as Peter was concerned he had four parents and he never realised, until many years later, that Dulcie was heartbroken to lose him.

In 1939 Dulcie and Geoff were in Dairen (in north-eastern China) and started negotiations to adopt a child; however, war was declared and the arrangements fell through as they had to return to England where Geoff worked at the Foreign Office.

Billie:

When Billie returned to Peking from school in England, she was very popular. The family liked Graham Duncombe, a young officer in the army, but to everyone's surprise, Billie accepted a proposal from the dashing Eric Thunder and they were married. Eric was a businessman who was known to enjoy betting at the races and kept up a flamboyant lifestyle.

Billie and Eric Thunder;

Noel Kirk (best man);

June Watson (flower girl);

Joyce Henning & Suzanne Fowler (bridesmaids)

At first they enjoyed life and Billie had a baby – David Stuart Thunder. But all was not as it seemed. Eric had been taking money from his clients to feed his gambling and he was arrested and tried. While he was in prison Billie gave dancing lessons to earn a small living and she dutifully stood by her husband through the scandal.

Billie and David

The Howell family never forgave him. Zou Zou remembered a dance where someone said to her, "Ah, aren't you Eric Thunder's sister?" She replied: "Certainly not! My sister had the ill fortune to marry him and has been far more loyal to him than he deserves."

It was said that sometime after Eric was convicted he was transferred to a gaol by boat and that on the journey he managed (or was allowed) to get to the deck and jumped overboard and drowned. However this was quite untrue and may have been contrived to hide the shame of a divorce. Billie and he were divorced. After his release Eric went to Australia where his step-mother Helen Thunder was living. In January 1942 he was recruited into the Australian army as a Private and he rose to the rank of Sergeant. On 28th December 1943 he was killed in action at Shaggy Ridge in the Philippines.

All came right in the end when she married Graham Duncombe when David was about seven. David took his step-father's surname.

Zou Zou:

Zou Zou continued to draw and paint once she returned to Peking. Having spent time in England she now saw China in a new light.

Erh Tiao Hutung
Peking

our house in Peking 1933

The Southern Heavenly Gate on the Summit of the Sacred Mount.

Dragon on the edge of a sluice on the Tungchou Canal

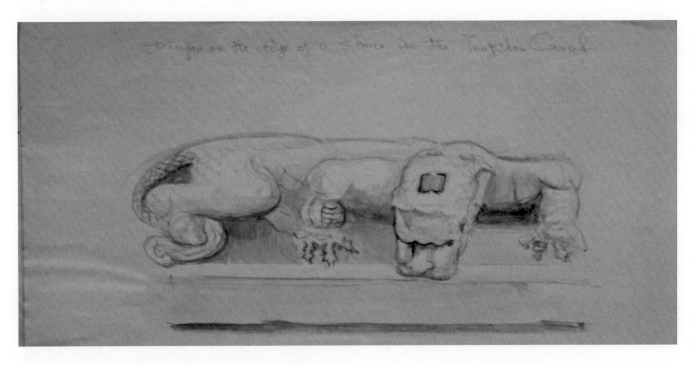

Dragon on the edge of a sluice in the Tungchou Canal

Portaits of family kept her busy in Peking.   Here are her mother and Arthur Dunn (Gladys's third husband).

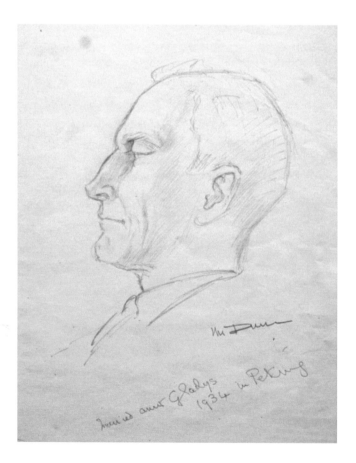

- And there were other portraits:

59

In Peking there were the usual social events. A photo shows her and Joan Tubb, a good friend, dressed up as the Princes in the Tower as depicted in the painting by Millais.

Left:
Zou Zou and Joan as "The Princes in the Tower" by Millais.

Right:
Hans Semmler in Peking
22nd March 1935

Zou Zou loved dancing. She was travelling by ship to China when she met a strong, handsome Austrian called Hans Semmler. On the voyage there were dances and entertainment. He was a very good dancer and as they danced she became aware that the other people had cleared the floor for them and applauded them when the music ended. She said whenever he met someone he clicked his heels and bowed slightly in a very Germanic manner.

He had a nasty scar just by his shoulder joint. He told her that when he was a boy he had lived on a farm. He had been playing in the barn and had slipped on the hay and landed on a pitchfork. The tine had gone straight through his shoulder. He carefully pulled it out and went back to the house where he bound the wound up as best he could without alerting his parents. He said he dared not tell his father because he would have been beaten for playing in the barn.

Hans proposed to her when they reached Peking. She liked and admired him but she refused him because, she said, he was so very serious and correct that she would not have met his expectations.

She said: "*What a strong character he was! I could never have married him because he would have been too protective and jealous, but I did admire him.*"

Hans Semmler

Flight Lieutenant Gilbert Bartholomew came to Peking in 1933. He was sent by the Air Force to study Mandarin Chinese. He was a good scholar and achieved high marks in his exams. While in Peking he joined in the British social scene. It was at a dance that Zou Zou and he "saw each other across a crowded room, and that was it!" as my mother told me later. When he called on the Howells a few days later he was announced by the Chinese Boy as "Mr Bathroom".

Soon they were engaged. He gave her a ring with a square setting of diamonds with a Chinese jade central stone. The Chinese jeweller gave him a note assuring him that the stones were indeed diamonds.

The wedding ring was a thin gold band with "Gilbert 12-10-35" engraved on the inside.

The Howells loved him. They were C of E and Bart was a committed Roman Catholic. Zou Zou said that he was so good and kind that she thought, "If it is good enough for him then it's good enough for me." She agreed to convert and to bring her children up in the faith with him. He and Zou Zou were married twice – once at the British Consulate and then at St Michael's Church, which Zou described as the "Roman Catholic Cathedral" in Peking on 12th October 1935. Zou Zou was 24 and Bart was 32. Joan Tubb was bridesmaid and Marjoribanks[1] (pronounced Marshbanks) was the best man.

---

[1] *James Alexander Milne Marjoribanks, diplomat: born Edinburgh 29 May 1911; CMG 1954, KCMG 1965; ambassador to the European Economic Community, European Atomic Energy Community and European Coal and Steel Community 1965-71; Chairman, Scotland in Europe 1979-90; married 1936 Sonya Stanley-Alder (died 1981; one daughter Patricia Baillie Strong); died Edinburgh 29 January 2002.*

Dulcie, Willie and Lionel Howell, Gladys (Dunn), Marjoriebanks, Joan, Gilbert, Zou, Gwen Howell and Cobbles Danby (behind), young woman, Dulcie Danby with Peter Larkins, Arthur Dunn, Billie with David, and RAF friends behind.

The reception was held at the family home 18, Erh T'iao Hutung.

Before long it was time for Bart to return to England for a new posting. He was to go home on military craft and so she took a civil passage on the H.M.T. "Dorsetshire" on her own and arrived before he did.

The first thing she had to do was go to Wimbledon and meet his family: his mother, his sister Agnes and his brother Francis, who was a doctor (later working in the Sudan). She was received rather coolly by Mrs Bartholomew and was not prepared for her rather strict, unbending religious views. She learnt that Bart had had a "good Catholic girlfriend" for many years and inferred that they were disappointed that he had married a "Non-Catholic". When Zou Zou pointed out that she had converted, she was told that that wasn't really the same, so from the start the relationship between the in-laws was difficult.

Above:
Bart and Zou Zou relaxing in China - 1935

Left:
The Bartholomew family:
Gilbert, Clara, Francis and Agnes
c. 1930

Zou Zou's story: Married life

As a new RAF wife, Zou Zou moved from posting to posting with her husband, staying at different houses owned by the RAF close to various aerodromes.   She had been used to this as a child and found it no hardship but her favourite place was a thatched cottage in Pewsey where they stayed not long after returning to England. The cottage had a garden raised above the road behind a stone wall. It was a beautiful cottage and she was very happy there.

When they were first married they were able to enjoy some leisure time together. Zou Zou remembered going to the countryside with Bart. They had a holiday near Betws-y-Coed. He liked fly-fishing and so they went together and she quietly sketched while he fished. She recalled that his mother had said she and Alfred had usually holidayed apart and that it was good to get away from each other from time to time – a strange idea to Zou Zou.

In April 1937 Zou Zou wrote a jubilant letter to her mother and father. The writing is huge with capitals, underlining and exclamation marks:

> *"O great news!!*
>
> *I'VE GOT MY MINIATURE of Gwen INTO THE <u>ACADEMY</u>.*
>
> *O Mother and Father isn't it wonderful XXX*
>
> *I can hardly write I'm so excited – When I opened the letter I hardly dare look – I got a free ticket to the preview on April 30th and it also is a season.*
>
> *O I am so happy I wept bitterly!! I did.*
>
> *O aren't you happy too?*
>
> *Everything happens at once – Gilbert's exam, then promotion, then the new job as P.A. to C.A.S. and then we get a wizard flat and then buy our own furniture and now this – O I can't write any more, I'm so excited.*
>
> *I'll write again soon.*
>
> *Lots of love*
>
> *Zou X"*

Willie joined the Royal Air Force as soon as he could after leaving school. By 1938 he was a Pilot Officer. Gwen and he were married 15th January 1938.

The miniature itself was kept by Gwen but unfortunately it was stolen with other small valuables from her flat in Queens Gate Terrace in the 1960s.

During 1936 Zou had suffered a miscarriage. However, in February 1938 their first son, Gilbert Lionel, was born. Her pregnancy made it impossible for her to travel to her brother's wedding.

She and Mary Evans (neé Sjobeck) had continued writing to each other ever since their childhood friendship in Japan. Now she wrote to Mary in America:

From Milestones, Barlows Lane, Andover,
24th July 1938:

". . . I enclose a few snaps of my son!! I've been meaning to write, but I don't believe I have since he was born. He is now nearly 6 months old and so cute – he laughs and tries hard to talk and has discovered he can suck his big toe! Which he thinks is a huge joke."

He was the first Bartholomew of that generation and therefore was a favourite with Agnes and Mrs B. (as we called her).

Mother said that Bart was absolutely delighted. He always wanted a big family. Before he had his own children he used to go to all the children's parties at the RAF bases and help entertain.

She regretted that for his short fatherhood much of his time was taken up with the extra official duties and distant postings necessitated by the war, which meant he hardly knew Peter until the boy was six years old. He also could be quite strict with his own children

Zou continued to draw and sketch. Gwen Howell, who was still composing songs with piano accompaniment, sent her a lullaby[1] for the new baby.

The year after Gilbert was born Europe went to war.

---

[1] Gilbert Lionel's Lullaby is in "The Music of Gwen Howell" book. ISBN 978-1-9163044-0-6

Zou Zou's Story: The War

On August 25th 1939, just a few days before the declaration of war, John Francis was born. He was premature but, although small, he was quite strong. Agnes visited and brought white and red flowers. The nurses tutted and took them away quickly. Zou Zou told me: "Nurses are as superstitious as sailors; they saw red and white without other colours as a sign of a death!" Agnes and Mrs B were insistent that the baby be baptised as soon as possible and he was taken away and baptised within a few days of his birth while Zou was still in bed in hospital.

For part of the war the family was in Andover and for a time they took a house in Millway Road. It was a nice house but the garden had been neglected. Peter was born in that house in May 1941. With three small children Mother had help. A girl came in to help with the washing and housework. After a few months in the house, Mother became aware of a few "cold spots" – places where sometimes it felt bitterly cold. She told the story many times and in 1977 she wrote it down.

The Garden with no Roses - Written by Zou Zou in 1977 -

This is a ghost story – a little sad but quite true.

At the end of September 1939 my husband was stationed at Staff College in Andover. We managed to find a semi-detached, three-storey house larger than we really wanted. It had been redecorated throughout, but the garden was in a shocking state. We were just settled in when my husband was re-stationed to Norfolk. No wives or family were allowed so we decided I would stay where I was with our two young children aged twenty months and five weeks· I got a young girl called Pauline to live in and help me·

It was on my husband's first leave that we first noticed unusual things· He and I had motored up to Wimbledon to see his mother· On our way back we were caught in an air-raid, therefore arriving home later than intended· I found that Pauline had bolted the door and she made sure it was us before she would open it· She explained that earlier someone had walked up and down on the gravel outside and tried the doors several times·

One day after shopping I was putting things away in the kitchen when a doorbell rang loudly· Pauline went to the front door but came back saying no one was there· I looked up at the bell indicator and was surprised to see it was bedroom 1 ringing· I ran upstairs to my room and stood amazed to see the bell-pull which hung from the ceiling over my bed was swinging violently from side to side·

A few days later I had put the children to bed and it was half-light· I went down to the kitchen and found there was no coke in the boiler so, picking up the bucket, I opened the back door· Outside there was a porch and facing it was the coal shed with coal on one side and coke on the other· I opened the shed door and was about to go in when I had an awful feeling that someone was in there — I could feel them looking at me· Then coal started to slide down as if someone had moved· I dropped the bucket, slammed the door, locked it and fled inside the house· The shed had no windows so whoever was in there was locked in· I would leave them till the morning·

Unfortunately I was upstairs when Pauline came in from her half day out· Seeing there was no coke, out she went and unlocked the shed and then did what I had done only she left the shed unlocked· When she got

70

back to the kitchen she heard footsteps on the gravel outside so whatever it was it was gone. I say "whatever it was" because often I would hear those footsteps - sometimes outside the kitchen, sometimes at the front and sometimes at the back of the house by the drawing room. Sometimes the door handles were turned hard this way and that. Several times I crept upstairs to look from a window but no one was to be seen.

Then a very strange thing happened. Again it was Pauline's evening out. I sat and sewed and listened to the wireless and my children were in bed asleep. At about ten pm I heard the front door open and close, I heard them bolt it and then run upstairs two at a time. Thinking Pauline was home early I got up and went to put the kettle on for a cup of tea. To my surprise the hall light was out. I switched it on and went upstairs. I looked everywhere - no one was upstairs at all. The children were fast asleep. I went down feeling puzzled and looked at the front door. It wasn't bolted. Half an hour later when Pauline came in she said she had not been in before.

After the Battle of Britain was over, my husband was sent abroad. My third son was born in that house in May 1941. By the time he was 18 months old Pauline had been called up and I was alone.

I had put the children to bed. With the blackout I used as few lights as I could. However, the upstairs hall light was on and at the bottom of the stairs the drawing room door was ajar, the light shining through. The downstairs hall light was not on. The stairs turned at the top and then went straight down to the drawing room on your left and the dining room on your right. I came down the stairs and in the half-light I saw an old lady standing by the dining room door. She was white-haired and pale and the square neck of her long black dress was white. I saw her plainly. She was small like me but a bit on the stout side. I saw all this at a glance and stopped dead on the stairs but she disappeared. After this I tended

71

to put the light on to go downstairs. It seemed whenever I forgot she would be there again, standing quite still looking up at me.

There was a WAAF called Vera, who used to come twice a week on her days off and spend evenings sewing with me. One evening I remember her going out to the cloakroom to try on some 'unmentionables' she had been making. I heard her switch on the cloakroom light but, the drawing room light being on and the door ajar, she didn't use the hall light. Then I heard a scuffle and she tore through the hall. As she came back into the drawing room she straightened herself up. Though she said nothing I wondered had she seen the ghost.

It was a week later that she came again and this time she said "Is this house haunted?" I asked "Why?" I wanted to know what she'd seen. A few days before I had been to the local priest to ask if he could exorcise the house but he had laughed at me and said I was nervous living alone which I was not. It was no good because, even if he agreed to do it, if he treated it as a joke it might make matters worse. However, Vera said she had gone to the cloakroom and switched on the light. She put on the garment leaving the door open. As she straightened up, she saw an old lady dressed in black watching her from beside the dining room door. When she looked again the woman had gone.

A few days later I had more proof. I went to see if Gilbert, who was by then four, was asleep. He was lying on his back holding the sheet over himself rolling his head from side to side. He had done this before but had not told me why. I was worried and sat on his bed and told him he couldn't possibly go to sleep if he did that. I talked to him for a bit and then at last he said, "Mummy, I don't like the old lady." I asked calmly what old lady and he frowned and said "I don't know. She comes into my room and walks across to the window and looks out, and when I talk to her she doesn't answer and then she goes away - and then sometimes I hear whistling round and round my room." He described her as old, wearing black and always going to the window and looking out across the garden. I told him not to worry, she was alright. Then we talked about other things and he went to sleep. I was shaken by this and surprised that she didn't disappear for him.

Sometimes, while standing in the upstairs passage, one could hear voices arguing in the attic rooms.

Another strange thing happened one night when I went to bed very late around one-thirty. The bathroom was above the kitchen and overlooked the porch, coal shed, garden shed and an outside toilet. Together they formed a long brick building. Everything was quiet until suddenly there was an unearthly row. It sounded as if two tramps were in the shed having a fight. I could hear watering cans being flung around and things falling and crashing to the ground. The noise was really awful but then all was quiet again. I was quite frightened but I had no telephone so I could do nothing until morning.

The next morning I saw to the children's breakfast and when they were settled I went out fearing I'd find an awful tramp laid flat out dead in the shed! I held my breath and opened the door. Everything was neatly in its place, not a thing out of order and the watering can where I had left it – not a thing had been touched.

It was 1943. I had been in the house for four and a half years mostly alone. It was getting on my nerves and I was now sleeping with a night light for my ghost was not always appearing in the same place. I would wake with a start and feel she had been standing over me. Once I went to the linen cupboard to get my baby a clean nappy and as I reached inside she was standing beside me. I screamed and turned on her. She stepped back into the corner of the stairs and vanished slowly from feet to head yet I didn't see her features clearly.

I was talking to the next-door gardener and asked him who had lived in the house before us. He told me that three, rather reclusive ladies had lived there for twenty years or so. One was a semi-invalid and blind. She was, however, quite well-off. The second lady was a companion and the third was her sister-in-law. He said the house had been very dirty and when the workmen came to redecorate after the old lady died they found the cellar was knee-deep in old open food tins and the garden had been so bad that a bulldozer had been used to clear away the brambles and ivy. The three of them kept to themselves and their only visitor was the old lady's brother who lived in an alms house and was always bothering her for money so that in the end she wouldn't let him in. He would walk up and down outside trying the doors.

One day one of the ladies called to the gardener asking him to help them as the blind old lady was ill and had fallen out of bed. They could not lift her back. He went in to help and was left a few moments alone with her. She caught him by the hand and said, "Please tell me is my garden full of roses?" He said he knew she was dying and he hadn't the heart to tell her that her friends had deceived her, so he answered, "Yes, beautiful roses." She died soon after that and where the other two went I do not know but I do hope, if they are alive, they realise what they did, for when my small son saw her so clearly she was at the window, gazing on the garden which I had by now cleared, planted a lawn and a vegetable garden. I could not get flowers to grow as the tall pines on the south side shaded the garden. Only one small wild rose grew and thrived at the edge of the lawn.

When my husband came home from abroad I told him I would like to move and told him this story. He didn't believe in ghosts but he knew I wouldn't make it up. However, on his first night home my second son, John, cried out in the night. I had been asleep and being used to doing everything myself I started to get up. My husband stopped me and said, "I'll go." So he got up and opened the bedroom door and found he had left the hall light on. John slept across the hall, his door being at the bottom of the stairs to the attic. When he came back he said, "John's alright now but he has just asked me, "Who was the old lady that just passed my door. Was it Grandma?"

We left the house in 1943. I wasn't frightened but I must say I didn't like it and was glad to leave the house and garden with no roses.

The house still stands in Andover and whoever lives in it has built a garage to the side. My daughter and I parked our car outside just to have a look at it a couple of years ago. My son Peter, now 36, was born in the house. I often wonder who lives there now. The garden is nicely kept and it looked as if the people were happy there. Perhaps the ghost has gone or perhaps some people see ghosts and some don't.

She wrote to Mary from *"Pinewood" 44, Millway Road, Andover*
26ᵗʰ September 1940

". . . Gilbert is on active service somewhere in England.[1] I'm staying here with two babies and I've got a girl to help me with them, she sleeps in so I am not alone. · · · · · Honestly you'd be surprised at the calmness of everybody · · ·

I wish it was all over and peaceful – being separated from Gilbert is awful – I try not to think about it, anyway the babies keep me busy. Gilbert is huge now, though only 2 ½ he looks over 3 – he wears jerseys and grey flannel shorts and looks most grown up! John is a darling little chap – very fair – his hair is almost white it's so fair and he has large brown eyes.

John (1yr 7 months)

[1] In 1940 he commanded Squadron 13 during the Battle of Britain and bombed Berlin. This was the usual expression used in letters whether you knew where they were or not.

Did I tell you I got two miniatures into the Academy this year – one of

Billie and the other of a Mary Barry-Power. I was most thrilled. . .

Billie has just got engaged to Captain Graham Duncombe of the Queens

Reg. He is very nice and all the family are very pleased about it. . . . "

Ursula Cox had remained a friend of Zou Zou's since they shared a flat in Cheyne Walk as students. It was during 1941, soon after Peter was born in Andover, that Ursula came to stay. She was in need of her friend's help. Her family had all but disowned her because she had become pregnant. She had an elder married sister, Isobel Curry, a twin sister, Cicely, and a younger set of twin siblings, Barbara and Peter. She became very ill with what may have been pre-eclampsia and was confined to bed and then rushed to hospital where she died in July 1941. Zou Zou was distraught, her own baby only seven weeks old and any hopes for her friend cruelly dashed. She was told that the baby also died. Isobel had her daughter, Jane, at about this time and she always wondered whether in fact Ursula's baby had survived, but Jane was a few months old when Ursula died.

Zou Zou found it very hard when Bart was away and the in-laws visited. Agnes was teaching and, according to Zou Zou, she must have taught for a couple of terms in almost every Catholic junior school in the south of England! She got a job in Norfolk so while she was away she sent her mother to Zou's house in Andover to be looked after there. Mrs Bartholomew had made it quite clear how she disapproved of Ursula and in addition she upset the girls who were there to help. Ronnie, who came to help, had a sunny personality and a good sense of humour and she soon became a good friend of Zou's. She had many anecdotes about Mrs B in those days! This was a particularly hard time with the bereavement, the new baby and Bart away in the war on "special duties" in Turkey. Zou Zou wrote to Mary:

Pinewood" 44, Millway Road, Andover
5ᵗʰ June 1942

". . . Gilbert (my husband) is abroad and has been since Nov 1940. He

has just been promoted to Group Captain. We have three sons Gilbert

John and Peter – the latter, my husband has never seen (yet) and he is

just over a year old now.

Willie and his wife are abroad in S. Africa they have a daughter born on 8th May this year. Mother and Dad are still in Peking unfortunately. . . ."

Zou Zou and Bart decided that while he was on leave in 1943 that they would look for a house of their own to buy. One of the factors to consider was that it should be close enough to Wimbledon for Mrs B and Agnes to visit but not to stay! The house they decided on was "Chessington Cottage", 39 The Avenue, Worcester Park. It was a short walk from the railway station – a direct line to Wimbledon. He was then sent to Chungking as British Air Attaché to China for the rest of the war. Chang Kai-Shek later awarded him the Cloud and Banner medal for his work there.

Ronnie came and helped look after the children while she waited to see if she would be able to join the WRAF. She married an Air Force Officer called Gordon Dick. She had so loved looking after the three Bartholomew boys that she called her first son John after our John. The marriage didn't last and Ronnie later married Eric Ratcliffe although Mother always said that their son, Philip, looked very like Gordon!

The house was in a group of about three pairs of similar houses built around 1850. Next door, 41, was a mirror image of "Chessington Cottage". It had for a couple of years around 1896 been the home of H. G. Wells and his second wife. His novel, "Ann Veronica", is set the Avenue. That house was empty, damaged and pulled down during the war.

"Chessington Cottage" was a large Victorian house in a beautifully stocked and laid out garden of about half an acre. There were oak trees at the western end of the garden, fruit trees, a large lawn and an avenue of roses on tall poles up the centre of the shrubbery. Mr and Mrs Whiting had made it beautiful. There were plenty of rooms for the children and for visitors. The house cost £2,000 and they borrowed some of that on a mortgage from the solicitor, Mr Owen. I think they bought the house through Mr Yeo at Birtles Estate Agents. We would often meet him in the town and say hello. (Mr Birtles was Merrial Webb's grandfather and she lived opposite us in No 40, the big red house. She became a good friend of mine.) While my father was stationed away, the family lived in Worcester Park. They were there during the blitz.

It was safer than the centre of London, but many bombs fell around Worcester Park. There were a couple of small round bomb shelters made in the garden – the bases of which later became small ponds. The Wise family next door (37) had a large concrete shelter in their garden. Mrs Wise was the local Air-Raid Warden. Mother never closed doors at night – you leave all doors wide open so that if the walls and ceiling fall in there is a way out. The doorways are the places most likely to withstand collapse.

During 1944 a bomb blew out some of our windows and the ceiling-rose in the front reception room landed squarely on the table below it with a large part of the ceiling. The roof too suffered badly and had to have tarpaulins stretched across it. Gilbert remembers standing in the downstairs hall and looking at the sky above him. However, the family stayed living in the house with an internal metal cage bomb shelter in one room.

She managed very well although the house may have looked almost uninhabitable at one stage. She remembered sitting by the fire in semi-dark with the windows all blacked out. It was night and the children were in bed and she was listening to a thriller on the radio. She heard what she took to be Gilbert out of bed going along the hallway to the toilet. A few moments later she realised that Gilbert wouldn't have been wearing boots and the footsteps she had heard had been. Nothing had been stolen, however, so all was well.

She told me that when the sirens sounded, if you were unable to get to a shelter, you should lie on the ground so that flying shrapnel would be less likely to hit you. She said she had been on Worcester Park station once when there was a raid and she had remembered the drill but found herself rigid and unable to move. So she stood there with the explosions around her. As she looked at the pavement in front of her a hole appeared in the tarmac – she cupped her hands together to show the size of it: "It was just where the small of my back would have been had I lain down like they said you should."

From 1943 until 1946 Bart was in China. In the spring of 1945 Bart was able to fly home from China for a visit arriving in Poole on 20th March. The war was all but over so on 22nd April they flew out together as passengers on several B.O.A.C. Sunderland aircraft and a C.N.A.C. Dakota back to China. The trip took several hops, stopping in Augusta, Cairo, Habbaniya, Bahrein, Karachi, Calcutta, Dinjan and Kumming – finally arriving in Chungking on 8th May, V.E.Day.   She was very happy to be reunited with him but said she regretted missing the victory celebrations in London having gone through the whole war in England. They had been separated for several years.

The boys were left under the care of Mrs B and Agnes whose own home had also been bomb-damaged.

She wrote to Mary in America describing the time in Worcester Park when the bombing was intense and the "doodle-bugs" were falling on London:

From   Chungking, China
18ᵗʰ June 1945

"Dearest Mary,
I am in Chungking with my husband, having left the children with my
mother-in-law at my house in Worcester Park.   My husband is Air Attaché
here and has been here for two years and has just about a year to do.
It's a most frightful place and takes all ones energy away I loathe it, but
Gilbert and I have been separated since 1940 and I thought it high time
we were together.   Now that there is no danger from bombs I felt I could
leave the children.

We had a pretty grim 1944!   The house being blasted twice – the
first time in February by a bomb which blew out the windows and my
front door.   I have been living alone most of the war.   I had a "companion
help" just after Peter was born but when he was 18 months old (John 3
and Gilbert 4) she was called up.   Since then I've not been able to get

80

help and lived completely alone - With sirens and air raids it was grim. Fortunately my next door neighbour came in when the raids were bad and she wasn't on warden duty. Anyway the windows were patched up and the door mended and then the V1s started!! I'm afraid we happened to be in what they called "Bomb Alley" and they came over us all the time or fell short - it was simply frightful - not a moment's peace day or night. When the "companion help" was on leave she came to stay so I wasn't alone. The day the V1s started I'd been in London to see Willie and his wife and on my way home the train was about at my station when the siren went. The carriage was full, no one moved or seemed to take the slightest notice - but I remember feeling quite sick. The siren always upset me. Anyway, just as we drew up at Worcester Park a man in the carriage said "There it is, look!" and it was coming straight for us - people got out of the train and I was about to, the thing went off and I was blown almost back into the carriage - guns were going - God! It was awful - then there was silence and I took to my heels and ran home as I knew my friend was alone with the kids - when I got in I found she'd put them to bed early in the shelter - she told me that John had had a fit - but was alright now and asleep. From then on the beastly things kept on coming.

Next day my "daily" never turned up and I heard her house had been bombed and badly damaged - the person thought she had been killed. I couldn't go out to find out as I couldn't leave the kids, Ronnie went shopping. That night we put the children in the shelter to sleep and brought a mattress down to share. We put it on the drawing room floor next door to where the children slept. The "all clear" sounded and we felt as if we could breathe - we went and had a quick hot bath getting back into blouses and slacks (we were in them for a fortnight) Anyway, we got down stairs and it was then - 11:45 - 17th June (just a year ago) the siren went off again and the guns and then before the siren had stopped the V1 was above us and the engine stopped. Ronnie and I put our heads down and then there was an awful noise. Everything seemed to fall and crash around us, then suddenly I saw the sky and the tail light of another V1 that passed over us and then crashed. We leapt to our feet – the air was full of plaster and soot – we coughed and choked and got to the children, tripping over furniture and plaster which had fallen – I said "Are you alright, Gilbert?" and his little voice came back: "Yes. Was that an air raid?" and then "Peter and John are still asleep." I said "Good! You go to sleep too."

And then Ronnie and I went outside and looked at the house – it looked pretty grim but it was still standing, so we just went back to bed. Next morning we had to wash and scrub everything before we could eat any breakfast – just covered in plaster and soot. However, we did manage and then the bell rang and six wardens were there to help clear up the place. You've no idea what it was like, Mary, not a window or frame left – some ceilings down (but not all, thank God) four plaster walls down – doors blown right across rooms – the roof hadn't a tile on it! Cornices blown off bits of furniture and my 6-foot shutters which had been closed had blown down and one was outside in the garden, the other hanging like a see-saw on what was left of the window frame. My glass cabinet had crashed down with the top touching our mattress.

It's going to cost £500 to get the place straight again. Thank God it's all over. You in America will never know what it was like; you're lucky. It was awful to watch young children going through all that hell and one could do nothing. John used to turn pale green at the sound of a siren and his teeth would chatter and he'd say in a shaky voice: "I'm not frightened, they're our soldiers guns aren't they?" I got away into the country after a fortnight of the V1s because of John. Gilbert, though he didn't appear to worry, began to run a temperature up to 102 F for no reason. One tried to keep the war away from them but it was no good, other children would tell them about the V1s and V2s. · · · · "

With the end of the war Bart came home at the end of March. A month later he and Zou Zou and returned to Chungking to complete his posting.

News from home and uncertainty about when Bart was to leave Chunking brought Zou Zou home again in October. Peter had been admitted to hospital with problems breathing. Mrs B said he had swallowed a cherry stone but in fact it was a bad episode of asthma. They had been warned to be extra careful and vigilant should Peter develop a cold. A neighbour said that Peter had been seen cycling up and down The Avenue with a streaming cold in the rain. The doctor told her that he had not expected her to see Peter again. She never entrusted any of us to Agnes or her mother again except in dire emergency.

Peter on his tricycle

Billie and David had been in Singapore and were taken to PoW camp but I believe were sent home before long. Zou Zou's cousin, Colin Ford, and his mother were also set free because Colin had sleepy-sickness (narcolepsy) from which he died in 1945.

But Zou's parents were still incarcerated by the Japanese in Weihsien Prisoner-of-war camp near Peking. Lionel's elder brother, William May Howell, and his second wife, Lena, were with them. William died one Christmas in the camp. Life in the camp was not easy: there were starvation rations and everyone had to work to maintain some sort of normality.

Even when the Japanese were defeated, the prisoners, for diplomatic reasons, had to wait for the Americans to free them. Bart was in China at the time and he was also present at the Surrender of the Japanese in Hong Kong. He was able to meet the Howells in Peking shortly after their release. They returned to Peking to try to resume life there, but all their property remained in limbo - the Japanese returned everything to the allies, and then the Chinese confiscated it! After some time, Gwen and Lionel returned to England without anything much of value to show for their lives' work in China. Both of them were thin and worn out by the experience; Lionel was almost blind in one eye from an injury caused by a Japanese guard striking him and he had heart trouble.

We had an oil painting of Patrick Norris in the house – even when John was young it was said he had Patrick's eyes. They were travelling on a train and the boys were talking about the return of their father. When John said, "Daddy's coming home." Gilbert replied, "He's not your Daddy, your Daddy is the one in the picture!"

Throughout the war and for a long time after it, Mary (Sjobek) Evans kept in touch and sent small parcels from the USA. Some of these went adrift, probably stolen en route, since they contained clothes, nylon stockings, books, toys, peanut butter and sweets unobtainable in England.

In her letters to Mary Evans, Zou Zou writes quickly and fluently as she thinks - without considering how to express some things more accurately. I can hear her voice in the letters; where she is upset she exaggerates in order to get her point across. Mary was a good friend and they wrote regularly. She was someone Mother could turn to when things were difficult and to whom she could get things off her chest when she was worried, and she could express her worries without fear of the family being offended.

When Mary died, John Evans returned a batch of letters that he found she had kept. It is notable that one of the people she wrote to on the very day of Bart's death in 1949 was Mary. She also wrote to her mother and father and sisters and to Mrs Bartholomew and Agnes. They would have received the letter a few days later, although her parents were horrified to hear that news on the wireless the day he died.

Gilbert and John c.1945

84

Zou Zou's Story: Post-war.

From Chungking, China
16ᵗʰ August 1945

"Dearest Mary,
So it's all over, isn't that wonderful· · · · Chungking has been sending off
crackers and shouting for joy and doing all sorts of things with search
lights· The government will move soon and then the embassies so I will fly
home· · · · · "[1]

Bart was away in Hong Kong for a week in September representing the British Ambassador at the Surrender Ceremony.

Meanwhile she had spent some of her time painting the local scenery:

CHUNGKING
China
1945.

View from bed room
window

The Hsinkai, South bank.
Chungking 1945.

T. M. Bartholomew

29ᵗ June 1945

Ann Sean - 1 Tien Lin
Qinzine

F. M. Bartholomew

On 4th October Bart accompanied Zou on an RAF Dakota and then a Halifax as far as Calcutta. She flew on to England and he returned to Chungking.

In England, Gilbert and John both started school. For Gilbert, starting school in 1943, it had been a new school every few months as the war progressed and as the family moved with different postings. John's first school was The Ursuline Convent primary school in Wimbledon where he must have started in 1944. Mother said that after he had been at the school for over two years, the teachers sent home a reading book and Mother discovered that John could hardly read and didn't know the difference between A and E. She went to see the Sister in charge and complained that they should have been doing more to help John. The nun said: "Ah, yes, but John has been to so many different schools and each time he has moved his education has been disrupted." Mother said, "That's true of Gilbert, but this is the first and only school John has attended." She said that she watched as a warm blush crept up the nun's neck and her face reddened and she almost felt sorry for her.

The relief of war's end was tempered by all the work that had to be done and the worries about family. Bart was still in China. The house needed extensive work and improvements it had to be done and arranged by Zou Zou.

From "Chessington Cottage", Worcester Park
10th January 1946

"Dearest Mary
Your lovely parcels arrived on Xmas Eve. · · · Peter insisted on wearing his
"American Pyjamas" straight away and showed them proudly to the
doctor. Poor wee Peter was in bed at Christmas with asthma. On the
23rd he started to cheer up and take an interest in everything – though
he was off food for over a week and has lost a bit of weight. He's up and
about again now. · · · · My husband's due home this May, thank goodness
– 5 ½ years this was his sixth Christmas away.
I flew home in October – left Calcutta on the 7th and was home on
the 10th! It was a tiring journey, but I enjoyed it – flew all the way
home on a "Liberator".
Willie and his wife and little girl came to tea with me on the 23rd
Dec. He has been awarded the A.F.C.

I'm glad your brother is safely home. I'm sorry not to have seen him and your friend Jeffy Lee. I somehow wonder if my sister-in-law frightened Jeffy Lee, for she answered the phone (I was away with the children). She is enough to frighten anyone. We don't get on at all together. . . ."

From "Chessington Cottage", Worcester Park
25th April 1946

". . . John is over the mumps and the other two are all right . . . today we are out of quarantine.

I'm completely browned off. I was expecting Bart home in May and have just heard he will not be home till July – that makes it six years abroad (all but 3 months) and he was away from home before that stationed in command of a bomber station during the Battle of Britain!! So browned off is putting it mildly.

Bart has just flown up to Peking to see my parents and I'm just longing to get letters telling me about it all and how my parents look[2]. Yes, my father went straight back to Peking and opened up his business again "Stocks and exchange Broker". They say it's all changed and the Chinese are not so pleasant – my father is claiming for all the things they've lost – but it seems that loss of business the government refuse to compensate. . . .

. . fats, sugar and soap are short with us. . . . There is no fruit in the greengrocers to buy – all meat is rationed except liver which you get once in a blue moon and then only if you're there on the dot. Fish – if you queue and wait ages even then they may sell out . . .

Now for a bit of advice, Mary!! Never have 3 children – have two or 4 or 6, 8 or 10!! But never an odd number – I find that when they are three together one is always left out and then there is trouble – but when they are two or a friend joins them all is well and they play together beautifully. Now don't ask me why I've not taken my own advice – the answer is above!! . . ."

---

[2] They had just been released from a Japanese internment camp at Weihsien

From "Chessington Cottage", Worcester Park
1ˢᵗ October 1946

" · · · Cheer up about housekeeping; I'm sure you're jolly good really· I was absolutely shocking when I first started· I used to put the veg on to boil, go off and play the piano (or try to) and forget completely about the wretched things and once I forgot completely about lunch and poor Bart arrived home to find me reading a very exciting book – I've improved now· · · · ·

We all got mumps – I got them too – first John and then just the very last day we could catch them, Gilbert went down and four days later I got them· It wouldn't have been so bad if Peter had had them too but he was fine and kept on running off down the road to play with a friend and I had to put a scarf round my head and go and find him· It ended up by me going into hospital and my sister-in-law being fetched to mind the children· When I came out the builders came to finish the war damage repairs to the house and the mess and muddle was terrible – in the end he walked off without finishing and I had to find someone else to finish off· It's been an awful worry and during all this the Air Ministry kept putting off Gilbert's return home· He was to have arrived on May 18ᵗʰ and then they said July and now October· His relief is supposed to arrive in Nanking today, October 1ˢᵗ – I wonder!!

We have been married 11 years on 12ᵗʰ Oct and I was 35 last Saturday – isn't it awful!

'Fraid Peter still has asthma· He is just over an attack – the worst I've ever known him have· I sat up all one night until 4 a·m· poor little chap· I've got a new doctor who is going to try injecting Peter against it (Didn't know they could·) · · · "

From "Chessington Cottage", Worcester Park
6ᵗʰ February 1947

" · · · My husband got home on October 29ᵗʰ (1946) and got leave until 12ᵗʰ January· He is in command of an R·A·F· station Tern Hill in Shropshire now and I hope will be able to come home fairly often· It is hopeless to try moving about from one station to another with children –

especially these days when you are lucky to have a house. It would be crazy. Tomorrow my eldest son is nine years old!!

John had a very bad attack of tonsillitis just before Christmas and will, I'm afraid, have to have his tonsils out this spring. The doctor suggested I take him away to the seaside - to Margate. Well off we went, John, Peter and I - the weather was beautiful but cold and we spent our time on the beach collecting shells and one day took a bus to Canterbury to see the cathedral. After six days it snowed. I stuck it there for another two days and then came home - it's snowed ever since. I love this weather, provided there's enough coal and coke to keep the house warm . . ." [3]

Mary continued to send packages to the family for years to come; we probably all remember the Harrods parcel every Christmas with tins of fruit, fruit juice and salmon. She was Mother's very best friend: having met in Japan when Mother and she were ten and seven, they had been pen friends ever since. Mary and John eventually came to England for the first of several visits, when Mother was at Chilston Cottage.

Almost every letter began with long thankyous for parcels of food, clothes and toys. Mary was very generous and aware during the war of the rationing and then later of my mother's more stretched circumstances. She always sent something at Christmas and often in between.

Mary's side of the correspondence, at least as long and rambling as Mother's, has been lost. She had her own troubles: finding they could not have children, she and John adopted a boy, Bert, (named after Mary's brother Albert) and then a girl, Pam. After that they exchanged photographs (snaps as Mother calls them) of the children. I remember reading one of Mother's letters as she wrote it and commenting on the use of "awfully" or perhaps "frightfully" in her text. In the 1930s they may have been normal parlance. Mother smiled and said she liked to make the letter sound as thoroughly *English* as she could, so these anachronisms were tongue in cheek and used especially for an American reader.

The children collected shrapnel from the garden and were able to play on the plot next door. In the house beyond that lived Dr Dene. He was a pathologist, a very glum-looking,

---

[3] The winter of 1947 was the appalling with temperatures down to -21C in Bedfordshire. Snow drifts built up and there was no let up for 55 days. It lasted from 22nd January until 17th March. When the thaw came there were floods.

solitary man who never acknowledged you when he passed in the street. Once when the boys were small and climbed the fence to look into his garden he told them to go away and Peter, fascinated by the face of the grumpy man commented, as small children do, "You've got a nose like a strawberry!"

Dr Dene's house was surrounded by tall dark trees and in the early sixties he sold the plot for development and moved away. After he left, a couple of tame crows were around for a few weeks so we knew he had had some friends after all. The group of houses built on the plot were named Dene Close after him.

Dulcie and Geoff had also returned from China and now lived in Cheam in the house previously belonging to his parents. The family were able to see each other fairly often and letters were exchanged almost weekly.

Having been separated for so long, when Bart was stationed at the Advanced Flying Unit in Morton in Marsh at the start of 1947, the family went with him.

From Officers' Mess, R.A.F. Station, Moreton in Marsh
3rd September 1947

"Dearest Mary
· · · I am expecting a baby this month on 25th and I am hoping it will be a girl and I was wondering if you would honour her or him by being the Godmother?
As you see by the address I am up living near my husband's aerodrome. The quarters are not too good, but it's nice being together. We are living in the ex W.A.A.F. officers' mess. My house at Worcester Park is left in charge of Mother and Dad who arrived back home just about eight weeks ago · · · both look awfully thin. However, I got the doctor round and he has given them priority milk and eggs rations which is a help – two pints each a day and three eggs per week. Already they are looking better.
· · · · · I wonder where I shall be in 1949. Hope I shall be in England and able to see you and have you stay with us. Bart may be sent as Air Attaché somewhere else abroad. · ·

· · · *The children are in their 7th heaven here – we gave John a rubber dinghy for his birthday and near this house is a water tank in case of fires. It's being used by officers for bathing and my kids sail on it all day long and are as brown as berries. They manage it awfully well. Gilbert has gone off to France with his Aunt Agnes to visit Lourdes. They ought to arrive there tonight and will be back about the 10th. I should love to go there – did you see the film? I didn't but wish I had.*

I'm calling my daughter Elizabeth – I'm not sure what name to call the child if it's another boy. I like Roger but my husband likes Hugh. · ·"

24th September 1947

"My dearest Mary,
Please excuse the pencil but I am in hospital. My fourth son was born on September 16th at 1:55 BST and weighed 7 lb 1 oz. I was very sad at first that I had not had a daughter, but he really is a beautiful baby and so good and content. We are calling him Michael Cyprian: The 16th Sept being St Cyprian's Day and Michael because we both like the name. Gilbert, John and Peter all approve of him and look so huge against him. They all go to a little country school run by nuns about five miles from here in Chipping Camden. · · "

From Moreton in Marsh
11th December 1947

"Dearest Mary,
· · · · *The children are all invited to a children's party at the aerodrome. Usually Father Christmas arrives by plane, so it ought to be quite fun. I'm taking Michael too. I do wish you could see him, he is so sweet and such a jolly baby – you'd love him. He has the rosiest cheeks and bluest eyes – his hair hasn't decided yet what colour it will be, but I think very fair, though some people swear it is going to be red. I shall send you a snap as soon as I can. I want to have all four boys taken together. If I do I'll send you a copy. It won't be long before Gilbert is as tall as me – already he takes shoes and gloves I can wear.*

Both my sisters went up to see the Royal Wedding[4] and I believe they both had quite a good view. I couldn't go but wouldn't anyway because I can't stand crowds."

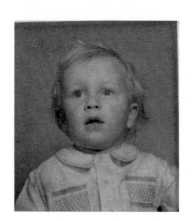

Zou Zou with baby Michael

Mother often mentions Michael specifically in her letters to Mary in America because Mary was pleased to become his godmother.

From "Chessington Cottage", Worcester Park
22nd January 1948

" · · · Everyone says how beautiful Michael is – he is four months old now and such a jolly little chap. He tries hard to sing – but only one note – you only have to say "Sing, Michael." And then sing to him and off he goes on this one note!!

---

[4] Princess Elizabeth and Philip Mountbatten

I'm feeling very lonely - Bart is still up at Moreton handing over the station to another unit and then he hasn't any idea where he is to be

stationed - so I'm back here with just Peter and Michael. Gilbert and John went off to boarding school on the 19th January to St Peter's in Guildford, Surrey. It is a new school - this is the first term - so all the boys are new. I do hope they will be happy - I am waiting for their first letters - they write on Sundays. . . . .

My father isn't at all well - they had an awful time as P.O.Ws and it's telling on him now. He is so frail. Mother seems strong enough though awfully thin and full of nerves, always on the go instead of taking things easy. A Harley Street doctor examined his eye and says nothing can be done; an operation would not give him back his eyesight. He says the blindness was caused by a blow (which a Japanese soldier gave him knocking off his glasses.) Dad's quite cheerful about it and his other eye is all right, thank heaven. . . . . . Willie is up in Manchester - his little girl has started school which she loves. It's such a pity to have only one child. Billie lives near Guildford. Her husband is abroad just outside Port Said (of all horrid places). It's time he was posted home - He has been abroad for almost 9 years!! Except for six months just after the war. . . . "

Generally Zou and Bart agreed on the way to bring up children and both of them were loving, firm and proud of their boys. Mother said:

"We never had arguments except once, when Gilbert and John were at St Peter's School in Merrow and they and another boy 'ran away'. I laughed at this; it showed a certain lack of respect for unnecessary authority that

I often felt myself. I could imagine my little boys running away. Bart was mortified saying 'How dare they run away when I am spending good money getting them a good education!' That made it seem funnier to me!"

From "Chessington Cottage", Worcester Park
18th February 1948

" · · · Bart has been re-stationed to Driffield, Yorkshire and we expect to be there two years. I'm a bit fed up about it, though it is a nice station with good quarters and only 10 miles from the sea, but so far north. I shall hardly see any of the family unless they come to stay. · · · "

However, his posting after Moreton in Marsh was changed and he was actually sent to Hullavington.

From "Chessington Cottage", Worcester Park
29th June 1948

" · · · My Peter has just come out of hospital today. He had to have his appendix out. I was so worried about it. He had got so thin, bad tempered and wouldn't eat. I brought him home just before lunch this morning and I must say he is eating well, is a much better colour and seems rid of his temper, so I am happy he will put on weight and be alright now. The sea air will do him good.

How are you getting on with your house? Is the kitchen very modern – with a refrigerator – you know like the ones you see on films – they say Americans are way ahead of us in their kitchens.

We are all well – Michael is a darling, so good and always has a smile for everyone. He stood up at 8 months and has two teeth. Gilbert and John seem to be really getting on at boarding school. Their holidays start on 13th July to Sept 13th. We are going down to a quiet seaside place called Wittering and have taken a bungalow there for a month. · · ·

Bart is in command of the Empire Training School in Hullavington · · He gets home most weekends. It's not much of a family life and the

96

petrol allowance, if used for this would only get him there and home once in three months! Isn't it absurd? So he comes by train – trains are not good either – Now I'm grumbling again! · · · "

Mother had been given the choice of Peter having his appendix out or leaving it to get better. She hesitated over whether he should have the operation, but an acquaintance told her she knew of a child whose mother had thought it best not to put the child through it. The boy then died of a burst appendix.

Then Bart got another exciting posting.

From "Chessington Cottage", Worcester Park
12th December 1948

" · · · We are off abroad again in March· Bart is to be Air Attaché to Turkey and this time we are all going – children and all·   I am looking forward to it· I can't imagine no ration shopping and as much sugar and milk as one likes – oh, it will be heavenly· · ·
I had a lodger too once and never again· Only my lodger was a spinster of an awkward age and thought everyone was against her· She objected to me writing to my husband! (He was abroad then) and banged about at night waking the children – running the hot water off till none was left and doing such spiteful things – in the end I had to be cruel and firm – I told her the date she was to be out of my house and said if she wasn't out by then I would pack her things myself and put them out – so I did and that was the end of her – I gave her five weeks to get out so I was very fair and if I hadn't been firm, I'd have her yet·
        Young Michael is walking all over the place now, he is such a good little boy and so friendly and always cheerful· He went to his first party yesterday and joined in all the fun and you should have seen him when balloons were given round· He jumped about and shouted with joy and excitement – everyone laughed and thought he was sweet· · · "

A five-year diary started in January 1949 gives some insight into the events of that year.

Zou Zou's Story - 1949

The Five Year Diary

The diary has only a few entries. It is a "Five Year Diary" and starts in 1949 with the first few entries in my father's hand and these are recorded in the biography "Bart's Story".[1] The later entries are in Zou Zou's handwriting.

1949

January 1st

At home in Worcester Park pending posting to Turkey as Air Attaché.

January 9th Sunday:

My birthday. Mass and communion at 8. Mother came over for the day.

(He was 45)

There are entries in the diary about preparations for the posting - packing cases, car, trunks, house in Ankara, passports, clothes etc., as well as notes as to where he was going on current RAF business looking at new aircraft that might be put into service.

On 3rd March they set off. They went via Dover, Calais, then by train to Marseilles where they joined the SS Istanbul for Genoa, Naples, Piraeus and finally Istanbul on the 10th March.

By May there are no more entries by my father and only a few in my mother's hand.

May 5th 1949: Mother writes:
Atlay Kemal Menderes gave dinner in honour of Gilbert and me.

---

[1] "Bart's Story" ISBN 978-1-9163044-2-0

May 20th :

Peter 8 years old - Sgt Scott gave him his birthday cake - had Maude children to tea. I had to go up to the Embassy. We wives met our husbands there after "presenting of credentials".

May 24th but also recorded on June 6th

Peter made his first communion - we all went, even Michael and Mr Porter. Little Dixie girl was also taking her 1st communion.

May 28th:

Went to buffet at Leak Ministers - dreadfully grim - came out and couldn't find our car - found in the end we were looking for the wrong one!

June 9th:

Cocktails with Sir Noel and Lady Charles (the Ambassador and his wife) in honour of the King's birthday.

Bart and Zou Zou with Mr Porter at a cocktail party at the embassy in Ankara.

Mr Porter had been employed by Bart as a tutor for the boys while they were in Turkey. Mother said Porter had taught before but she thought he had had some trouble with alcohol and Bart was giving him a chance to rehabilitate and recover his reputation. Peter recalls learning the flags of the world from Porter but not much else. He may have been better at teaching the older boys.

Mr Porter had been, as Gilbert learned later, a protestant vicar. He had converted to Catholicism and therefore had been out of work. This was a chance to make a new beginning. The family were surprised when his wife came and saw him off since they were unaware he was married.

June 10th:

Went to dinner with Minister of Foreign Affairs, M. & Madame Necmeddin Sadak.

June 26th:

Cocktail given by Michael Everett to welcome Mr and Mrs McNab.

Living in Ankara was interesting and the children seemed to thrive. They got a dog, 'Whisky', and a donkey, 'Dinky', as pets. The donkey ate the apricots from the tree and then very delicately spat out the stones.

There were wild tortoises. One day Mother heard a commotion – someone crying out. When she investigated, she found that the boys had collected a number of tortoises and corralled them together; one of the larger ones had cornered another and was banging into it. The victim was squealing. The tortoises were freed. Later in Worcester Park we had a pet tortoise called Said after the cook in Turkey.

Peter remembers: *"In Turkey one day we went for a picnic and drove the Standard Vanguard out to a very pretty village in the foothills of some mountains.*
There was a derelict house on a hilltop overlooking the Turkish village with some bushes around it. There were sheep grazing and a river flowing past at the

bottom of the hill· A beautiful scene, but one of us found some bones under the bushes· Dad thought it could be a sheep but mother confirmed that the bones were a human child's· Dad conducted a brief burial service and we moved down to the river· He explained the Greeks had dominated parts of Turkey and had been thrown out, that must have been why the beautiful house overlooking the village was derelict and the child unburied· There are still whole Greek villages in Turkey abandoned and left to rot, and the Turks will not go near them apart from allowing sheep to graze there· And yet there were a few Turkish children with blond hair who had Greek blood in their veins, (according to Dad·)

That same day Gilbert and John wanted to catch a water snake in the river, and were stopped by Dad who said it was almost certainly venomous· I am sure there were photos of us paddling in the river that day· Michael was dressed in white with a big floppy hat."

On another occasion they were driving through the countryside and some boys started throwing stones at the car. "Stop the car!" Mother ordered. She got out and strode over to the ringleader, a boy of about eight. She told him firmly (in English) how naughty and dangerous it was to throw stones at a car and, since he only spoke Turkish she reinforced the message by spanking him. Then she got back into the car and they drove on.

"Do you know who that boy was?" asked Bart laughing. "He is the son of the Chief Policeman!"

Mother always said that she thought both Bart and Maude had some premonition of what was about to happen. "He told me he had been woken by the howling of wolves, and he said, 'I've made a will.' And I said, 'Oh, let's not talk of such things now!' I just wish I had asked him where he had left it. It caused so much trouble not finding it later."

A Turkish artist, well known and whose drawings of Ataturk were used on some Turkish stamps, was commissioned to do portraits of both Bart and Zou Zou. They agreed that hers should be the first one done. It shows her in a green blouse with red and white flowers on it - the very one in the photo of them with Porter.

August 13th Saturday:

Sat for Saip Tuna and my portrait was finished.

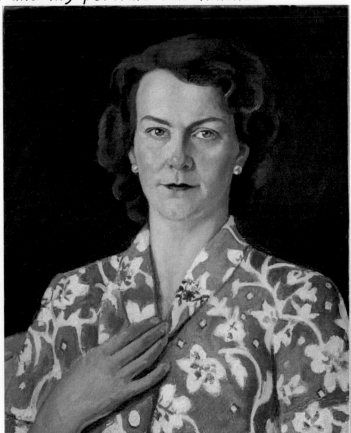

Portrait by Saip Tuna after restoration in 2021

There is no entry in the diary on Sunday, August 14th 1949. Bart, Burnand and Maude were all Roman Catholics so they went to an early mass and then set off to the aerodrome. The boys had hoped to go with them but had been left to sleep until it was too late.

In her letter written on the day to Mary she says:

"Dearest Mary,

My husband was killed in an air accident this morning - I was there when it happened and know nothing could have been done and it was all very sudden - that even I hadn't time to realise what had happened until after. The plane took off and then tried to re-land but went into the side of a hill. W/O Dow and I were there only a few seconds after and there was nothing left.

I expect we shall be going back to England soon. I don't know my plans. Everyone is being most kind, but we've only been here 5 months and don't know anyone very well yet.

My love to you both.

Zou."

Michael was with her when it happened; he says:

"Evidently Mother was holding me when the plane took off. Everyone stood watching and talking while it disappeared from view. I was perfectly happy; then, suddenly I got extremely distressed and started to cry loudly. A second or two later the smoke from the crash appeared in the distance. Mother was convinced that I had sensed the crash the moment it had happened."

Bart must have been killed instantly and with him two Turkish airmen, Wing Commanders Maude and Burnand and Flight Sergeant Whitworth.

In those days it was generally felt that children should not attend funerals and the boys did not. Mother often said that maybe that was the wrong decision as they never really said goodbye to their father. She worried that Gilbert had been angry not to have been allowed to the aerodrome to see him off and therefore felt they had parted on bad terms. She said that it was a long time before she realised this because, at eleven, Gilbert had already learnt to keep his feelings to himself.

Tuesday, August 16ᵗʰ:

State funeral – starting from British Embassy down to the Italian Embassy Chapel.

The funeral procession – pictured as it began from the Embassy – was a state funeral attended by British and Turkish troops, a military band and Turkish government officials and foreign ambassadors.

The banner from the wreath says "With love from Zou John Michael Gilbert Peter"

Wednesday, August 17ᵗʰ:

Mrs Baker and a few others came to help pack. The boys and I left Ankara by 9 p.m. train.

Thursday, August 18ᵗʰ:

Arrived Istanbul – stayed with Sir Noel Charles and Lady Charles – boys awfully good.

She kept most of the condolence letters and telegrams she received and dutifully answered most of them. They came from all the family, from many acquaintances in Turkey and from Marjoribanks and other people Bart had worked with.

There were letters from Mr Courtney, and the Vicar of Cuddington, Mrs Cook, Dr Philips, Anita Ardaillon, Mrs Wise – all neighbours and friends in Worcester Park. There were letters from friends: from Molly Martin and the sisters of Ursula Cox, from Dorothy Cafferata, Gervais Taylor's mother, Joan Tubb, Stephen Knight, Mrs Hook – a neighbour from Andover - and many others.

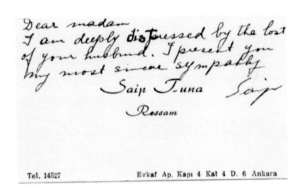

The artist who had so recently finished the portrait sent his card:

Longer letters came from Simon Maude's wife and from his mother and from Lewis Burnand's brother. Agnes sent a letter saying she had been in contact with Simon Maude's aunt who was a nun.

Friday August 19ᵗʰ:

Sailed from Istanbul 10 a.m.

She told me that on the voyage home she felt desperate. She leaned over the side of the boat and looked at the water; it offered a way out – a way to be reunited with him. "It was only my love for the boys and knowing how much they would need me that stopped me." Gilbert found her standing by the stern of the ship on the way home, she was crying and he asked her what was wrong, "What do you think?" she said.

August 25th:

John's 10th birthday – arrived Calais, crossed channel, arrived Victoria at 7 p.m. Geoff, Mother, Francis and Mrs Hogan were there to meet us.

She told me that it was only when she had been back in England about a month after the accident that she finally sat down and cried properly.

Bart's body was brought back to England and on 1st September there was a funeral service in Wimbledon followed by burial at Putney Vale Cemetery. While we lived at Worcester Park we visited the grave once or twice every year to plant flowers around it.

September 16th:

Michael is 2 years old.

No 39, The Avenue had been let out for a year and it took time before the family could return to it. Mrs Wise, a good friend and neighbour at no 37, offered to take them in when they got home. They stayed at her house until they found somewhere to stay for the longer term before returning to their own house.

September 22nd 1949

Moved into flat at 36, The Avenue.

Mr and Mrs Evans owned 36 and let out the upper storey and the family rented it. Mother said that Evans would regularly come home drunk and then shout at his wife and on occasions he hit her. Mother once went down and harangued Evans about his behaviour, giving him a good telling off – he was evidently better for a week or so afterwards.

September 28th:

My 38th birthday. Dulcie and Billie came over to tea and Geoff and Graham came later on.

On the 3rd October she wrote again to Mary in America:

"*My Dearest Mary,*

We are back in England. They rushed us back without delay. The state funeral was on 16th August and we left Ankara on the 17th the voyage home was ghastly, it seemed like months, not only a few days. We arrived on 24th August and I've been staying with friends and relations, but now have taken a flat at the above address until March when my own house will be free.

Gilbert, John and Peter are at boarding school – "Stonyhurst College" and they seem happy. It's a beautiful school up north near Blackburn, Lancashire.

I had my Bart brought home and he is buried near Wimbledon.

You've no idea how good the Americans were to us. The American Ambassador's wife took the boys off (the day it happened) and kept them busy, showing them films and I don't know what and bringing them home at 11 p.m. happy and so tired that they just tumbled into bed and fell asleep.

Another American whom I had <u>never</u> met took them out for a picnic and kept them all day – and yet another sent me 8 tins of milk for Michael on the voyage home. And last but not least an American plane brought Bart home for me – for nothing. By sea I would have had to pay £300 and by plane £50.

I thought I'd just like to tell you that, my dear Mary.

Love Zou Zou."

October 12th:
Bart and my wedding anniversary been married 14 years.

In October 1949 Zou's brother Willie, who was in the R.A.F., was badly injured in a flying accident. He was having tea at the Lancashire Aero Clubhouse opening when they asked him if he would do some aerobatics for them in a Tiger-Moth to round off their air display. The man who was booked to do it had said the weather was too bad! He gave a dashing display of aerobatics – low because of the bad weather. He came out of one spin just in time, but not out of the second one. He dived vertically, still spinning as he crashed at the side of the flying field. Rudder failure is what they blamed it on – it was not an R.A.F. maintained machine. Willie was in hospital for some time and then recovery was slow but apparently complete. News of the accident made Lionel ill again. Mother wrote to her parents urging them not to travel to Lancashire to visit Willie until he was a lot better.

36. The Avenue.
14.10.49.

Dearest Mother + Dad.

It's a miracle that Willie is alive. I was talking to Wing/C. Wise and he says he has never heard of a man coming out of a spin crash alive. He is in the accident Depot at Bushy Park. Try not to worry about not going up – it would do no good if you did – perhaps later on when Willie's a bit better you'll be able too.

I am thinking of going up to Stonyhurst, about 29th to visit the children + see the school – Mrs B. and Gywas too – I was wondering if that is anywhere near + I could go on + just visit Willie + Gwen. Anyway I shall write to Gwen + find

October 15th:

Went to lunch and tea with Joan Earl at Steatham, Mrs Tubb's flat.
(Joan Earl née Tubb had been Mother's bridesmaid.)

October 16th:

Went to lunch with Mrs Bartholomew and 11 o'clock mass.

October 17th:

Met Mrs Cafferata in town – lunch at Claridges.

Mrs Cafferata was an old friend of the Bartholomews – a good catholic and Gilbert's godmother. She lived in Stiffkey Hall in Norfolk which she and her husband had renovated and landscaped. They were there during the thirties at the time of the scandalous trial of the vicar, Harold Davidson. He had started on a career as an actor but having been ordained he became Rector of Stiffkey. He began to spend a lot of time in London engaged in social work and as chaplain to the Actor's Church Union in the West End theatres. He even spent time in Paris acting as chaperone for dancers at the Folies Bergere. He worked with the poor and down-and-outs and tried to help prostitutes return to a better way of life. There was little evidence that he had done any wrong. However, he protested his innocence and to raise funds to clear his name he became a seaside performer. He even did some lion taming, acting as Daniel in the lions' den in Skegness. Unfortunately he trod on a lion's tail and was mauled to death in 1937.

October 18th:

Epsom County Hospital 1:45.

Mother at first believed that her periods had stopped because of the shock and depression following the accident. She told me that she was always healthy when pregnant and suffered very little sickness or cravings (except for ginger biscuits) during pregnancy.

Bart had told her: "When we get home again to England we'll try just once more for a girl."

October 21st:

Susan and Margaret came to tea.

Violet Punnett was an acquaintance from Peking; she preferred to be known as Susan. Back in Peking Violet had once acted in the "Peiping Institute lo Fine Arts" Little Theater play: *"Flat to Let"* by Arthur Macrae. Lionel Howell had played the part of Lord Java, Gwen Howell was Minna and Miss Punnett played the part of Susan. It may have been this that gave her the idea of using the name.

She claimed to have introduced Bart to Zou Zou. It seems that he had first been interested in Susan herself, but, of course, he was a Catholic so she wouldn't have married him and therefore introduced him to Zou Zou! Violet/Susan later married Harry Langstone and they had one daughter, Margaret. When Margaret was a baby, Susan complained that she never slept at night and that she was at her wits' end. Mother took Margaret for a week to give Susan a rest. She said that for the first night the child woke and cried for attention but after a few days she got into the routine imposed on her and behaved beautifully and slept 12 hours in the night.

November 6th, Sunday:
Mother's 64th birthday (Gwen Howell aka 'Granada' was born in 1883 and was therefore 66 in 1949). Michael and I went to Shamley Green for the day.

November 7th:
Spent whole day at Mrs B's. She is much better but still in bed.

November 8th:
Went up to Turkish Embassy and saw their ambassador.

November 9th:
Dulcie came round early.

November 21st:
Letters from Peter and John.
Mr Evans very bad, terribly drunk. Mrs E. called me down.

November 22nd:
Paid rent. Dulcie came to tea.

December 14th
Went Christmas shopping in village, sent off parcels.
Wrote to boys.

December 15th

Shopping with Michael. in afternoon went to Bentalls.
Dulcie came round.

December 21st:

Went up in hired car, met boys at Euston 1:15 train. Dulcie minded
Michael. Peter Larkins came round with parcel from Mabel.

December 25th:

All went to mass at 8 a.m. then back to breakfast and opening parcels.
Tea with Mater and Agnes.

December 26th:

Mrs Wise took Michael for day. Dulcie and Geoff and I went down to see
Mum and Dad at Shamley Green. Boys went to Mater's.

Zou Zou with Anita, Mrs Wise and Mary in 1966

Mrs May Wise was our next door neighbour at no 37 The Avenue. She had been the local
Air Raid Warden during the war. She had three grown-up children: Stuart, Anita and

Mary. Stuart was in the RAF and sat on the Benevolent fund Committee at one time. He had an interest in UFOs and reports of them from pilots went to him. Anita was the widow of René Ardaillon and they had a daughter a few years older than me called Marguerite. Mary Wise was unmarried and lived down The Avenue in a flat in Orchard Court. All the family were good friends to Zou.

December 29th:

Mary Wise took boys to see "Treasure Island".

December 30th:

Left Michael with Mrs Cook and took boys up to London to Gamages and Hamleys.

Mrs Cook came to help with the house work and cooking. Later, when I was still very small, Mrs Garrity took over.

The diary was a Five Year Diary so Zou Zou continued to note things in it for the next few years.

The Five Year Diary and Letters – 1950s

1950

January 1st:
Went over to wish Mrs Wise Happy New Year· Willie is 34·

She wrote to Mary in America:

From 36, The Avenue, Worcester Park
2nd January 1950

"· · · Michael and Gilbert are the most like my Bart – in fact young Gilbert grows more like him every day, though Bart's eyes were golden brown and both Gilbert and Michael have blue eyes – a pity· I hope you approve of your godchild·

I don't know if I have told you or not but I am expecting a baby· They said about the 12th May, but I think it's more likely to be 12th April· If it's a girl I shall call her Elizabeth Jane – and if a boy: Hugh·

Gilbert, John and Peter seem very happy at Stonyhurst College there were no tears when I saw them off at Euston Station· Gilbert of course is getting quite old now – he will be twelve on 7th Feb, and I have been told by so many: "What a handsome Boy!" · · · "

On January 9th it would have been Bart's birthday and the boys went to 7am mass for Bart and then the family took flowers to Putney Vale Cemetery where he is buried.

Meanwhile Willie was still recovering and was moved to Headley Court Convalescent Home (RAF Headley Court near Epsom). This meant that the family could visit him. He was making good progress and was expected to make a full recovery.

May 6th 1950:
Elizabeth Jane born 3:05 a·m·

The name was predetermined. In 1947 my father had chosen Elizabeth Jane. "And it mustn't be shortened!" he said.

May 7ᵗʰ Sunday:

Moved into ward with 4 other women. Mother came to see me.

When I was born and the midwife told her that it was a girl my mother burst into tears. "Oh dear! Didn't you want a girl?" she asked.

They didn't put wrist bands on the babies in 1950. What's more the babies were kept in a separate nursery ward and brought to their mothers at feeding time. My mother tells me that they gave her a baby and she took one look and said: "This is not my daughter - I am not going to feed it." She was told not to be so silly, but when the others were given their babies another woman said, "This is Mrs Bartholomew's baby!" so they swapped and were happy. I could be a foundling!! The staff were a little insensitive too, telling her that her husband should register the birth, so she said: "I haven't got a husband!" which shocked them.

At around this time it was discovered that "blue baby syndrome" – where healthily born babies rapidly deteriorated and died – was caused by the mother having O-negative blood and antibodies managing to cross the placenta to destroy the baby's A or B cells, inherited from its father, in its blood. The antibodies first formed at the birth of the first child and so didn't affect that child, but could kill subsequent siblings. I suppose they tested her blood (O-negative) and mine (B-positive). The doctor came to see her and told her she should not try for any more children: "This is your first?" Mother was pleased to tell them it was her fifth.

From "Chessington Cottage", Worcester Park
9ᵗʰ May 1950

"Dearest Mary,
I'm in hospital at the moment and you'll be pleased to hear I have a daughter born 4:05 am (BST) on Saturday 6ᵗʰ May. She weighed 7lb 10 oz. I'm just longing to know what the boys think about having a sister. I mustn't spoil her, must I· · · ·

· · · now I have a "nannie" and she is looking after Michael until I come out – then I suppose they will send me a "home help".

The boys went back to school about a week ago so they won't see Elizabeth Jane until she is nearly 3 months old. I can't make out who she is like yet, though her nose and ears are like Barts. I think her eyes too will be brown – I hope so.

Well I must end and write a few other letters. Again thank you so much for your lovely parcel.

With love
Zou Zou."

May 9th Tuesday:
Dulcie came to see me.

May 10th Wednesday:
Got up. Mater came to see me.

Clara Bartholomew's children called her "Mother" but she asked Zou to call her "Mater" (Latin for mother). Zou found that almost impossible – it didn't seem natural. As far as I can remember she always referred to her mother-in-law as "Mrs B." We children didn't really have a name for her. Clara was born in October 1867 so she was 68 when Gilbert and Zou were married, 70 when Gilbert Lionel was born and 82 when I arrived. She was always old and distant, rather deaf and poor-sighted. When we dutifully visited them she sat in her chair by the window at their flat in Arterberry Road letting Agnes do most of the talking. She was never "Grandma" – possibly "Grandmother" - but definitely "Mrs B".

May 12th Friday:
Elizabeth one ounce under birth weight, 7lb 9oz – 7th day.

I was always told I weighed 8lbs when born but evidence suggests 7lb 10 oz – it could just be Mother's strange grasp of maths!

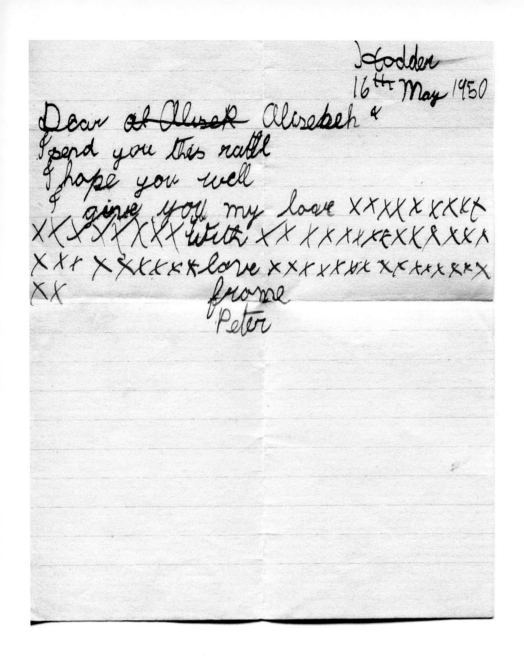

Hodder
16th May 1950

Dear at Olisek Alisebeh &
I send you this natll
I hope you well
I give you my love XXXXXXXXX
XXXXXXXX with XX XXXXXEXXRXXXA
XXX XXXXXX love XXXXXXX XEXXXXEX
XX   from
                    Peter

She got phlebitis in her leg and had to stay in hospital until 22nd May. There are no entries in the diary until 20th May where she writes: *"Peter is 9 years old – got Dulcie to send him a cake and sweets."*

Peter says that when sweets were sent to him at Hodder they were confiscated as being bad for boys.

He also said that when he had news that he had a new baby sister he had told one of the priests. The priest said, "Let me see: your father was killed in August." and proceeded to count the months on his fingers. Peter had no idea why.

May 22nd Monday:

Dulcie fetched Elizabeth and me out of hospital. Michael stood and stared at EJ; I think he thought she was a doll. When she moved he caught hold of her hand and said, "Nice hands!"

Michael, aged two and a half, when trying to say Elizabeth ran the sounds together and thus a pet name for me, Libbus, came into use.

May 27th Saturday:

Elizabeth Jane baptised. Stephen Knight godfather. Agnes stood proxy for Joyce – Dulcie drove them to the church – all came back to tea – I am still in bed with my leg.

Stephen Knight was a long-established friend of Bart's. They had been at school together. However, I had little contact with him. Joyce was Francis Bartholomew's wife but they may have been abroad at the time. They had three children: Clare, Anne and Richard. I believe Zou Zou was Richard's godmother.

There was lots of help available and family and friends visited and rallied round. Miss Birmingham was one. She had been friendly with the family during the war and had made cakes for the children but because of rationing the cakes had no sugar in them so although they looked wonderful they couldn't help but disappoint. She looked after Michael from time to time.

July 26th:

Milkman told me Mrs O'Connor hadn't taken in her milk for two days. Phoned and then went to see her. She looked awful and has shingles.

Margaret O'Connor lived at Orchard Court near the bottom of the Avenue. She had been one of the local people who had sent condolence letters to Turkey immediately they had heard the news. She had started her letter: "My dearest little friend, What can I say to soften your great grief?"

July 27ᵗʰ:

Went to see Mrs O'Connor. She is very ill and depressed.

Agnes came and took Michael out for the day. Had a plumber in doing the

WCs. Dulcie, Agnes and later Sgt Winchester came to tea.

The next day Mrs O'Connor was taken to Briarwood Nursing Home (at the bottom of The Avenue).

July 31ˢᵗ:

Boys come home. Agnes and Mrs B came over and had high tea ready when I got home with the boys. They had all grown especially G and P – train was early.

On the anniversary of Bart's death:

August 14ᵗʰ:

Went to mass with Elizabeth and boys. Left Elizabeth outside the church in her pram. Susan Langstone came to tea. Dulcie took us all to the cemetery.

It was quite normal in the 50s to leave a pram outside a shop or church where the baby might enjoy the fresh air and light. People used real prams for several months before putting a child in a pushchair. Our carriage-built pram stayed in the hall for years. I put dolls in it and hid things in the space under the board on which the baby's bed was made.

We would usually go to Putney Vale around the anniversary of my father's death and also in late spring. I remember the cuckoos calling from the trees around while we planted flowers around the grave.

September 16th:

Michael's 3rd birthday. Men painted kitchen woodwork.

The kitchen had cream woodwork. In the scullery off the kitchen, which held the gas stove, the sink and cupboards for pans and crockery, the woodwork for the cupboards and shelves was always brown. It may have been this that was painted.

To Mary from "Chessington Cottage", Worcester Park
26th October 1950

"Dearest Mary,

Just a line to send you the first snaps of Elizabeth – she is such a good baby and is beginning to notice everything – fancy she will be six months old on Nov 6th.

I have been meaning to write for ages but have been frightfully busy – I have had to have this house made into flats – I have the ground floor and the attic and the middle is another flat. It's quite nice really and I have let it to a Squadron Leader and Mrs Brown. They have a small boy the same age as Michael.

· · · My brother is out of hospital at last and home again. He limps rather badly, I believe, but has been given a permanent commission by the R.A.F. providing he passes his medical test in 10 months time. He will never fly again but will have a ground job.

Billie and Graham are still in Germany · · · Daddy is still very delicate – his heart is very bad indeed, the doctor says it is a miracle he is still alive. · · · On Nov 6th we are all going down by car as it is Mother's birthday – They live in Billie's small cottage. · · ·"

1951

On the 18th January Zou Zou's father Lionel Howell's heart finally failed and he died.

To Mary from "Chessington Cottage", Worcester Park
26th January 1951

" · · · I've got sad news too, Mary, my dear father died a week ago – 18th Jan· He has been ill for a long time – really ever since he came out of Japanese Prisoner-of -War camp· I think they made him work too hard and carry heavy things – his heart was so bad the doctor told Mother it was a miracle he was alive, but the last two years he has been in and out of bed most of the time and only able to go for short walks if the weather was good – which it seldom has been this last year· He died peacefully· Mother is taking it awfully well· Billie flew over from Germany and is with her now and I believe Mother will go back to Germany with Billie for a short stay·

Gilbert is now in long trousers and is beginning to look quite grown up – he will be 13 soon· John grows slowly and Peter is shooting up and is taller than John· John is 11 and Peter 9· They are getting on better at school and their reports are beginning to be fairly good·

· · · · · · I hope your husband won't be called up[1]· The news is very grave, but I hope it won't ever come to anything that will be the end of everything· It certainly is very worrying·

· · ·

The baby (Elizabeth) is growing fast· She sits up and takes notice of everything· She is awfully sweet now· We've had the most dreadful weather – too wet and damp to take a baby for a walk – it's a wonder she looks so well· · · "

---

[1] The Korean War had started.

April 8th – Boys went to early mass· Weather a little better· Children played in garden, very muddy – cellar flooded·

The cellar at Worcester Park had large slate shelves on which we stored apples from the garden for the winter. Nothing was kept on the floor because it was liable to flood. When they bought the house there had been a well in the cellar. My father had the whole floor cemented, covering over the well and leaving only a small drainage opening.

May 6th 1951:

Elizabeth is one· Stephen Knight called and gave her Brumas cuddly toy· Agnes and Mrs B came to tea also Jose Ratcliffe·

Jose Ratcliffe was the little daughter of the family renting our flat.

Brumas was the new cub born to Ivy the polar bear at London Zoo. I still have the pair of white bears: Brumas and Ivy. They are not conventional teddy bears. My mother made a jumper for Brumas and they were always my favourite toys.

To Mary from *"Chessington Cottage", Worcester Park*
9th May 1951

"· · · Michael is just over a mild attack of Chicken Pox· Elizabeth is teething but she is awfully good – she just adores Michael and the other boys· She has quite a lot of hair now and it's beautifully wavy (like her Daddy's) not like mine which was always straight as a poker!
Mother is in Germany now with my sister Billie·

I expect you're worried by this Korean War too – in fact more than us British – though we are worried enough· Why on Earth can't there be peace? Russia is the very devil· They are like a horrid spoilt child who won't see reason· Looks as though my children will never know what it is to be free of rationing and all the happiness I had when I was a child – What a lot of misery Hitler has on his soul – we are nothing to what some have suffered and lost – It's terrible to think of and now Stalin is trying to start it all up again – or is it all sham?

   Dear Mary, I hope your husband will not be called up again and that you can live in peace and happiness· · · · "

"Chessington Cottage", Worcester Park
14th July 1951
"My Dearest Mary,
You've no idea how glad I was to get your letter and snaps of the darling little baby you have adopted· He looks beautiful and so happy and funnily enough I think he looks like your husband · · ·

   Elizabeth is crawling everywhere and stands up and says quite a few words – She is really a darling with her blue eyes and fair curly hair (which I hope she will keep·)

   I hope to take the boys to the festival[2] these holidays I've heard that it is really good but that the food is an awful price and very poor – we shall take sandwiches·

   I had the 'flu quite badly when I got your letter and then went to stay with Mother for a fortnight· Just lately I went up north to have a look at Stonyhurst College the school my boys go to· It's a lovely school and such nice mannered boys· I liked it very much and enjoyed my stay·

   I do hope there will be peace in Korea· Surely we can live at peace even if we don't see eye to eye·

_____
[2] The Festival of Britain, organised to raise morale after the war.

I think prices have gone up everywhere. I pay my 'daily' woman 2/6 per hour – I can only afford to have her twice a week at 3 hours per time! That's fifteen shillings!! Isn't it awful!

Michael is fine. He will be going to school in a year's time. · · ·"

1952

To Mary from *"Chessington Cottage", Worcester Park*
22nd *January 1952*

" · · · Thank you for · · · that amazing book for Michael – he simply adores "Hoppie" – it's awfully clever. · · ·

I expect you enjoyed Christmas more this year with young Bert – children do make it more exciting. · · · · · Peter fell off his bike and cut his knee badly – I had to take him to hospital in a taxi and he had three stitches – and injections for tetanus and penicillin. I've spent the whole holiday taking him to have injections each morning – which puts one behind with one's work. Poor Peter he had a rotten time – and I was hoping the holiday would do him good – he is so thin and growing fast.

How are you all? I'm glad you are thinking of adopting a little girl, an only child is a rotten thing to be – what will you call her?

Elizabeth is awfully sweet now – she is very advanced for her age (20 months). She went to her first party the other day and thoroughly enjoyed it – joined in all the games and they say ate more than anyone else! Her latest word is "Fun" and when anything makes her laugh she says "Fun" – she tries to dance when the wireless is on. Michael was awfully jealous of her at one time, but he is better now – and she adores him.

My sister Billie and her husband are due home from Germany next month. It will be nice to see them again. Her son has just joined the army – has to do 4 months in the ranks and then goes to Sandhurst. (He would have been called up for National Service as was Gilbert.) He has grown such a very nice boy and nice looking – he loves army life. My boys haven't quite decided what to do – except Gilbert who says he wants to join the Navy. Peter shook me these holidays by saying he wanted either to go into the R.A.F. or become a priest. I hope he will do neither. He is only ten and changes his mind often. Gilbert will be fourteen this term – everyone says he is such a nice boy – I think he is too, but a mother is no judge.

I don't seem to have time to make friends or meet people – I suppose at my age(!) one doesn't. My boys' friends' parents live far from here, which is a pity as it would be nice to compare notes. The only person I seem to see is my husband's sister, whom I can't abide – she's so very narrow minded and doesn't like anyone and is always making trouble – I wish she would not come and see me – I seldom go there – it's always been so plain that they didn't really approve of me (Agnes and old Mrs B.) The brother is quite nice and I like his wife very much indeed – they are out in the Sudan. . . ."

This is the first time she puts into words the loneliness she was to feel from time to time throughout the rest of her life –

I don't seem to have time to make friends or meet people –
She was busy with her children and visitors always had their homes and lives to go back to. She said she no longer was invited to dinner with people because she would be a woman on her own and unbalance the guest list.

February 6th

King George died – no wireless only news.

To Mary *from* "Chessington Cottage", Worcester Park
4*th* December 1952

" · · · I'm so glad you have a dear little girl, she sounds like you with fair hair and blue eyes· I shall look forward to seeing a snap of Bert and Pam when you are able to send one· · · ·

I have the boys home on 17*th* December – I do love Christmas· I've managed to get a doll (that walks) for Elizabeth·, and I made a Noah's Ark for Michael and bought lead animals· It ought to keep him quiet for hours· Michael started school this last term and simply loves it·
· · · Willie is in London at Air Ministry· Since his accident he is more serious and looks older than he is · · ·Billie's husband has now retired from the army · · ·Dulcie lives in a flat in Cheam quite near me and often cycles over to see me· Her husband is at the Foreign Office· Billie's son is doing his 2 years service in the Army – they got him into Sandhurst but he didn't like it and left after the first term so now I don't know what he intends to do·

My Gilbert wants to go into the Navy and is at home now being coached· John and Peter are doing fine at Stonyhurst· John is very clever – Peter is good at art, music and poetry!!

Elizabeth can talk and understand anything one says· She is awfully forward for a child of 2 ½ years· She looks older too as you can see from the snap· She adores Michael but he gets annoyed with her at times· They are both very fair with blue eyes· Michael has very light eyes and he always takes beautiful photographs – he will have to become a film star!!

My mother is living in a small cottage with a Mrs Ibbertson (sister of the author, Sir Philip Gibbs) Sir Philip has just written a novel about

Mother's life[3] – he has made her a generation younger than she is but I found it very interesting to read.

· · · I'm sure you will find two children far less bother than one and being so close together they will be great friends and have more fun · · ·"

****

The early fifties were a terrible few years for Mother. The death of Bart in August '49 was only the start of several family bereavements. Willie had survived his flying accident but, weakened, died suddenly in 1956. Mother had great affection for her Dad, Lionel Howell. He returned from China ill from the deprivations of Weihsien, partially blind and with a heart condition that took him away in 1951. These were the three men in Mother's life that she loved above all others.

In addition Uncle Francis, our father's younger brother, who had been a doctor in Khartoum in the Sudan, was taken seriously ill and died in a nursing home in March 1953. Mother could not understand her mother-in-law's way of dealing with her sons' deaths. When Bart died, Mother hoped to give comfort by saying that he must have died quickly with very little suffering. Mrs B. said indeed she hoped it had not been so quick because he should have had time to repent all his sins and any suffering on earth would make his time in Purgatory less! When Francis was in hospital they visited him knowing that he had little chance of survival. Mother said she tried to be encouraging as she talked to him. She was then horrified when they were about to leave and Mrs B. said, "Now let us pray for the dying" and proceeded with some depressing prayers that they all had to join in with.

March 2nd 1953:

Francis Bartholomew died at 5:45. Funeral March 6th.

There is nothing more recorded in the diary.

---

[3] Lady of the Yellow River – published 1953 by Hutchinson & Co. Ltd., Stratford Place, London

Zou Zou's Story - The 1950s to 1964
Worcester Park

Illustration Showing "Chessington Cottage" by Zou Zou Bartholomew

The immediate worries on return to England involved sorting out finances because there was no will and, as importantly, working out what to do about schools for the children.

The RAF gave her a War Widow's Pension and also paid for the children's education. Mother had promised Bart to bring their children up as Roman Catholics. She felt personally unable to teach us the Faith since she herself had not had the full education in it. For that reason we were all sent to Catholic schools even in my case, long after I was obviously not practising. She got advice from her brothers-in-law, Graham and Geoff, and from the priest. Geoff suggested that a public school where the boys could board would be good for them, and they would probably enjoy it as much as he had enjoyed going to Cranleigh School when he was a boy. However, Geoff's experience had been that of a boy in a stable environment before the First World War.

There were advantages to this in Mother's mind: she told me that she was worried that a widow bringing up boys without a male influence might make them effeminate. She was so afraid that if she were to keep all her boys at home she might make them into "sissies". In addition the RAF would pay for the uniform, the travel to and from school and all the fees including books and full board. They only required the reports to be sent to them. In a boarding school all the food and heating costs would be included in the fees; if she really found herself in relative poverty, at least her boys would be fed. It was probably the local priest or maybe Father Barber (a friend of Bart) who suggested Stonyhurst and its junior department, St Mary's Hall, Hodder. These schools had a good reputation.

It took some time before Mother realised how badly treated the boys were at that school. She had expected them to be homesick and thought at first that that was all that was wrong. They had all had a broken-up education to date, being moved from school to school with different postings and in addition starting their education during the war. Once they were at the school she was reluctant to force another move. Boys at Stonyhurst were beaten for even small misdemeanours. It was the treatment of Gilbert that she first became aware of. Despite all the trauma of his father's death, the staff at the school were unsympathetic to the extent of being cruel. On visits she saw the buildings, which were very fine, and the pupils, whose behaviour was excellent.

Mother was very naïve when it came to sex - she knew there were "queers" but I don't think she had any idea about sexual abuse. She might have been worried about the beatings at school, if they had not been part of the normal "caning for misdemeanours" that her brother-in-law, Geoff Larkins, would have said were an unfortunate but normal and necessary part of school life. How badly advised she was!

Meanwhile life went on:
To Mary from *"Chessington Cottage", Worcester Park*
11th April 1953

" · · · I have had both Elizabeth and Michael very ill - they had whooping cough and measles all at once - the two things I most dread· However, they are both well again now· · · · Both my sisters have seats for the Coronation - I'm Cinderella!! I don't mind as I am just hopeless in a crowd and begin to faint · · · Luckily I got the 24-hour 'flu on a Sunday and Gilbert was home and able to cope with the children because I couldn't even stand up·

My husband's younger brother died suddenly on 2nd March - so now there is only his mother aged 86 and Agnes, who is a most difficult person to get on with· Francis leaves a wife and three children· Joyce his wife is very nice and easy to get on with - but we are both worried about Agnes, as when Mrs B· goes she has no one at all· She is a born spinster and most difficult and a very strict R·C· · · ·"

After Clara Bartholomew died in 1964 aged 96, Agnes, although still strictly following her religion, became rather more mellow. She maintained and enjoyed her independence and later leant on John and Michael as her nephews living nearest to her for some occasional help. She had her own car and her teacher's pension and a good social circle from within the church. She lived independently until only a few months before her death.

The boys continued at Stonyhurst for almost four years but during 1953 she became aware that all was not well. What alerted her to the mistreatment I cannot tell and maybe she didn't know all of it. She probably didn't understand and sought the advice of Geoff who did, and told her to remove the boys from the school immediately. She would have fiercely defended her children had she understood what was happening. She went to see Father Vavaseur, the headmaster, and I can imagine that he said it was all in the imagination and boys often seek attention and lie.

To Mary from *"Chessington Cottage", Worcester Park*
26th August 1953

" · · · I meant to write sooner only I had a row with the Rector of the boys' school. Not really a row – but he behaved in a very <u>rotten</u> way and so I told him as politely as one can be rude, what I thought of him and withdrew all my sons from the school and put them elsewhere. Gilbert is going to a local school. John to the "Oratory" at Reading and Peter will go there when he is older, until then he is going to a very nice boarding school in Banbury, Oxfordshire. To do this all on my own has been a great worry but everything is settled and I feel far happier than I have done for ages. I am certain I did right and to Hell with the Rector and his underhand ways!!! I will keep well away from Jesuit Priests in future. · ·

· · · Gilbert and I walked the Coronation route one evening. The couple in my upstairs flat minded the children who were in bed. It was fun – the decorations were not so elaborate as I had expected. The Mall was really beautiful – like a fairy scene – and Selfridges had a most beautiful coloured statue of the Queen on her horse, "Winston"· It has been bought by the Australians which is a pity· The people who did really good decorating were the poorer class in London round Enfield and Wandsworth· They had even twined red, white and blue round the iron railings and paper flowers everywhere and flags across the streets from house to house opposite· · · · · · · John was 14 yesterday · · · and just in the last week or so Gilbert's voice has started breaking! · · · "

Gilbert was sent to St John Fisher's in Purley and was able to be a day boy. John went to The Oratory in Woodcote near Reading and Peter to St Louis in Banbury. Both were boarding schools.

The rooms at Worcester Park were very big and Mother employed a decorator called Mr Skeggs to redecorate the main drawing room and the little ground floor bedroom that became mine when I moved out of her room. After we had had a few tenants using the upstairs, Mr Skeggs put in a partition to make the flat more self-contained. Mother called it a "petition".

The first tenants whom I remember were an Air Force man, with his wife and their two children, Jimmy and Sue, aged about the same as Michael and me. Mother once asked them babysit me while she went shopping. When she came back I was sitting at the top of the stairs screaming with my hands clenched so tight that my nails had dug into the palms. I don't remember it but I know that nobody ever babysat me again except Dulcie and that was fairly rarely.

It turned out that the wife had suffered post-natal depression and had to go to have electro-therapy. She used to shout at Jimmy – so much that Mother said if she spoke normally to the boy he didn't react because he didn't know you were speaking to him. I remember playing Cowboys and Indians with him in the garden, making bows and arrows from the bamboo that grew near the lawn. Michael said if the cowboy died he'd just fall in a heap but Jimmy said they were always spread-eagled and that's how you knew they were dead.

One day the wife gave Mother a large meat cleaver saying: "Could you look after this for me, please? I'm worried what I might do with it." Mother put it at the back of our shed and never gave it back. Mother wrote a long, worried letter to Mary in early 1954 about Christmas and about her tenants:

From *"Chessington Cottage", Worcester Park*
21ˢᵗ February 1954

"· · · We had quite a nice Christmas· Mother came for a few days and then on the 27ᵗʰ Dec the whole of my family – Dulcie, Billie and Willie met here with their spouses and Billie's son and Willie's daughter· B's son is a very nice boy and has taken up acting – which upset his step-father as he wanted him to go into the army – anyway he has got over his disappointment and David is doing quite well and will, I think get somewhere·
Willie's little girl is a funny child!"

In answer to this point Georgina wrote:
> *"I am sorry we did not see more of you when we were all children, and I am grateful that Zou had me to stay that time. For me it was unbearably exciting – I am afraid chiefly because of your brothers: I hardly knew what a boy was, but four of them together was too much for me. I was in agonies of shyness. Perhaps that is what Zou noticed when she said I was a 'funny child'."*

"Willie and his wife · · · though they are in London (for the past 18 months or more) they have only asked Mother up to see them once· I've been twice· He should by rights provide for my mother, as they lost <u>everything</u> in the last war and when Dad came home, his heart was <u>so bad</u> he couldn't even go for a walk on a slightly windy day and the last year was spent almost entirely in bed· But it was my eldest sister who had to suggest we all helped them out by giving so much per month – my brother agreed after <u>much</u> letter writing·"

Mother was aware that at this time Willie (Bill) and Gwen still had the RAF pay packet, while she was bringing up five children on a widow's pension. They had rent to pay in London but she had a mortgage and maintenance bills. Dulcie and Billie were both reasonably well-off and Mother felt that no one really appreciated how difficult making ends meet was for her.

Georgina replies:

"My parents never managed to buy so much as a country cottage. The best place we ever lived in was the tiny flat in Kensington Court, followed after my father's death by the basement flat in Queen's Gate Terrace, both chosen because they were the shortest distance from my day-school.
In this setting, the brighter spot seems to me to be my own happy family of three. I would assure Zou, if I were able, that we were indeed a happy family and shared great affection, humour and resilience to setbacks. My father and mother loved each other deeply, were always together, and made each other happy."

Georgina,
Bill (Willie)
and
Gwen Howell

Zou Zou loved her sisters and brother very much but she often felt almost trapped by her relative poverty and by her widowhood. She roundly criticises Billie for being unfeeling in one of the letters. But those letters were to a close friend who was not emotionally connected to the family and who was never likely to meet them again; Mother could 'let off steam' to Mary, whenever she was feeling upset, where she had to bite her tongue within the family and because of that her pen runs away with her. She had a much more volatile temper than was usually seen from the outside; on the positive side it made her able to stand her ground and insist on the rights of those she cared about. She could work herself up into a temper thinking about life's unfairness and writing to Mary would release it and make her feel better again. There were many times when I found I didn't have the skill to comfort her.

As for her relationship with Gwen, I think she was mildly jealous of the way she always managed to look smart and beautifully turned out. She once said: "Oh dear, I always feel so dowdy beside her!" I think that Zou and Gwen didn't really get to know each other until after they had shared those terrible tragedies. Then Gwen was often much more able to sympathise than either Billie or Dulcie and their friendship became much firmer and more understanding.

We all used to wear in hand-me-downs! I remember that Dulcie would often give me a dress for Christmas but otherwise friends and relations passed on clothes. Mother usually found she had to alter dresses given to her because she was only five foot tall. Even in the summer holidays I would alternate just two sets of clothes, and the RAFBF helped pay for school uniform.

Mother continues her letter to Mary:

The couple that have taken my upstairs flat are a queer couple, she is a bit peculiar - spent 8 weeks in a mental hospital before Christmas. She is one of those people that want to do away with their baby. At her son's birth she had to be separated from him and went to a mental home - then all went well and they went out to Singapore - where she produced a daughter - the little girl is now 2 years old and the boy, five. The girl can do no wrong and the boy is always at fault according to her - (most unjustly sometimes too.) I get on with Mrs W very well (although I shall be glad when they go) as one never knows what she might do next.

I always thought her so placid and easy going until she started her tricks just before Christmas. Said she felt so depressed and I laughed and said everyone does at times - but no she said she felt far worse etc. etc. - She went on for hours about herself and what she felt like!! At last she went to a psychiatrist and then went on for hours of what he said and she felt - she said she had to go for 20 treatments - would I mind her kids? So I did - it was only for about 1 or 2 hours - but the treatment went on and on and on for 3 months, 3 times a week - looking after her kids even for that short time was getting a bit of a bind - with five of my own rushing about too! Anyway she rang up one day from her treatment, said she was in an awful state and could I give Jimmy some tea (she had taken the small girl with her, as I had to fetch Michael from school and couldn't have managed two babies getting on and off busses -

136

Elizabeth and her little girl) Well I told her not to worry I'd give Jimmy tea and that was that. Six o'clock came so I bathed the kids and put them to bed – Jimmy included. Well just as I had done so, there was a knock on my back door and the doctor's wife from next door was there in a state – she asked where Jimmy was and was greatly relieved when I said "in bed".

She then told me, Mrs W had rung her up asking her to go up to London and bring her home as she felt she would throw herself out of the train if she was alone. I'm afraid I saw "RED" then (Mr W was up in Scotland) and I've a devil of a temper when it's roused. Mrs W had told me I was the only one to know all this and I found out she had told the doctor's wife the same thing and another friend of mine too. Anyway, to get back, I told the doctor's wife she was on no account to go up to London. (Mrs W is twice the size of us!) She said she'd ask her husband, the doctor, who ought to be home any moment and she departed. Anyway she returned and he had said just what I said – she wasn't to go – and he phoned the hospital and asked them to send Mrs W home in an ambulance. They didn't; they saw her to Waterloo and onto a train and she got home at 7:30 pm. The doctor's wife and I saw her to bed and gave her a sleeping tablet and a hot cup of tea and that was that. I was so mad I couldn't face her for 2 days – We get on alright and she doesn't know how angry I was. A few days later she was whisked off to hospital for 8 weeks – coming out about a week before Christmas.

Now she has taken a job and has some woman in to look after her children. There have been rows and though I don't listen, I'm sure her husband doesn't approve of her taking a job – she is nursing at Kingston Hospital and I'm sure the Matron does not know all about her or she would not have her there I'm sure. I think she is a fool – the marriage cannot go on like this. He earns quite enough to keep them in comfort (being an R.A.F. officer) half her earnings (£3.5.0 per week) goes to the woman (30/-) – which means all this fuss for 35/-. Her husband is off duty on Saturday and there he is stuck here alone with the kids and has to cook lunch. She told me last Saturday evening that when she got home all he had done was to light the fire, no beds made or anything. I laughed and said "O well men aren't good at house work!" I didn't think it dawned on her at all - she thinks of herself the whole time and I've noticed that since she took this job the children get on her nerves more than ever. I never hear them cry until she gets home! I shall be glad when they go - but I'm afraid it may be some time yet - but you never know with the R·A·F·

All my kids are fine and so much happier in their new schools. John is doing really well and came 2nd in his class. Elizabeth is growing so big and she loves dolls and keeps hers carefully, treats them just as if they were real. She also sings awfully nicely and is proud of her whistle - I'm afraid she has learnt (from the wireless) the whistle boys make when they see a pretty girl!! She and Michael are great friends but they fight sometimes - but Elizabeth adores Michael.

Your little girl looks so sweet. What a pity she and Elizabeth can't play together. It's amazing how much she looks like you. I hope you are all well - do they go to school yet? My Elizabeth doesn't. But so many people send their kids at 3 or 4 years - I think it awful. School is hard enough when you have to go at 5. I always hated it and at 16 I refused to return.

Gilbert was 16 the other day - everyone says he is the nicest boy - he is very quiet and is growing fast - especially his feet, takes size 10 in shoes, he is about 5 ft 6 inches or 7 · ·

138

In 1954 she wrote to the RAFBF telling them that she felt she and her family needed a holiday and asking for some help with the finance. She said:

"Despite care with money it hasn't been possible to go on a holiday since Bart died. I never go to the hair-dresser; I don't buy new clothes; I don't eat out at restaurants and neither do I go to shows; I haven't got a car and I don't buy any luxuries."

Stuart Wise, whose mother, May Wise, lived next door to us, was on the RAFBF committee. He said that at the meeting where the letter was read out, several members of the committee laughed and said they wished their own wives were so good. They granted her some money to take us away to the seaside in the summer. We went to Deal and stayed at a hotel visiting Dover and Deal castles, going round the Dover lifeboat and on a boat trip out to see the wrecks. It was a very good holiday that I remember well. Mother described it in one of her letters:

" – last holidays seemed to fly by – we had our first seaside holiday for five years! We stayed at a small hotel right on the sea front at DEAL, Kent. It was a dear little place – rather old fashioned and not too crowded – The three elder boys bathed every day, but it has to be jolly hot to get me into the sea! And I'm afraid the weather wasn't too good – We visited Deal Castle which is very small and unspoilt, Walmer Castle where Wellington used to live and Queen Victoria stayed there too

occasionally.   We also saw Dover Castle – unfortunately it started to pour with rain so we caught a bus back to our hotel instead of going down into Dover to see the ports and docks which Michael would have liked to see.

The hotel manager and his wife were such a nice couple and everyone said what nicely behaved children I had.   One nice old lady said "Of course the three elder children are not your own, you're far too young to have sons of that age!!"   We got quite well known in Deal by the time we came away.   One place we used to go for tea got to know us quite well and their cook came out of the kitchen to see us!!   I heard the owner say to him: "Here is the young lady with the large family again."

Michael started school at The Holy Cross in New Malden when he was five and then followed his brothers to their schools. He was only just seven in September 1954 when he started at St Louis as a boarder and he could have waited a year but Mother felt that while Peter was also there he would help his younger brother settle in.

Letter to Mary 12th October 1954:

. . . Now all the boys are back at school – even Michael is at boarding school now.   I sent him because the school he was at was a girls' school and when a boy is 7 years old he is too big to be at a mixed school being taught by nuns.   But my chief reason was that Peter is at this school. Next year Peter will go up to the "Oratory" where John is – so you see my reason was that Michael will have a whole year with Peter and so he will be used to the school by the time Peter leaves.   Michael has never been away from me before and though he is rather "homesick" he has at least got Peter there and so it isn't quite so bad.   Poor little Michael I do miss him.

Elizabeth is just over the 'flu.   She doesn't seem to miss Michael as much as I thought she would.   She will start school next summer term and Gilbert has one more year at school!   I don't know what he intends to do. He wants to be a marine and do diving and be a frogman, but whether there is any future in that – I don't know what he will do.   Anyway I must go and see Canon Byrne, the head of his school as soon as I can this term.

John is doing well, he seems to be the brainy one – coming first in maths (not like his mother as you well know at Mrs Davidges!) He is top of his class too. Peter is quite clever too but inclined to be lazy and dream – he is musical but just won't practise which is silly of him."

I still have Sq/Ldr and Mrs W upstairs – She has been all right lately and of all things has taken to nursing again at Kingston Hospital and seems quite happy – I get on quite well with her – though sometimes I feel I could SHAKE her till her teeth rattle! She is quite nice when she is sensible – I don't leave Elizabeth with her after your warning though I baby-sit for her often enough. They may go any moment now.

I thought of you with these awful hurricanes. Did you have any ill effects or is Newtonville too far away? · · ·"

At school Michael managed to avoid the sexual abuse but recalls:

"Peter virtually disowned me at St. Louis, but after a couple of weeks I had my own friends. There was sexual abuse there but I think Peter was probably left alone as he was one of the older boys (too risky – might talk) by the time he got there. Certainly some members of my dorm (7 – 9) were abused by the Headmaster, Mr R-B, on a regular basis, when he'd had a few too many beers.

I once got up in the night to go to the toilet which was opposite the dormitory door. Mr R-B came round the corner and beat me to it, so I waited, seated on my bed, the one closest to the door. When Mr R-B emerged he flew into a temper seeing me out of bed. He grabbed me by the arm and flung me over so he could spank me. My head crashed down on the bottom rail of the bed. I could have been killed or seriously injured. Instead of seeing whether I was all right he stormed off without checking me. The next day the right side of my head was out like a balloon. All the boys asked what had happened. Not one member of staff mentioned it. I was 8 or 9.

Mr R-B died of a heart attack while I was at St. Louis. We boys mistook shock for grief, I believe. I for one was not unhappy to see him go. I still remember the overwhelming smell of beer and cigarettes in his study where he would happily hand out punishment every minor transgression. Mr R-B used to dissolve in floods of tears during the "Stations of the Cross". I always thought, "What a hypocrite when you cause so much suffering yourself".

Mrs R-B was just as bad especially after her gin. After leaving school I occasionally got letters from Sarbie as she liked "affectionately" to be called asking me to visit her if I were passing. I never replied nor visited."

One thing I can thank my mother for that she taught me to observe rather than just look. She would encourage me to draw and pointed out that trees were not all the same green and their trunks could be grey or green not just brown. In the garden she would turn over a damaged leaf to reveal a caterpillar and knew the names of the different birds. She refused to teach me to read as she said it would confuse me, but once I could she encouraged me to use books to discover more about what I had observed.

In January 1955 Zou wrote to Mary to thank her for her Christmas parcel:

From *"Chessington Cottage", Worcester Park*

"My Dearest Mary,

I left writing to you until the boys had gone back to school, when I get a bit of peace and quiet!! John went back on 14th and Peter and Michael today. And I've been feeling a bit "browned off" so I'm writing to you as that will cheer me up.

Your parcel was lovely as usual. I have not had time to cut the black skirt shorter - but otherwise it is a perfect fit - thanks for the lovely nylons too hankies and gold and silver braid and the gold belt. The boys loved the Fax game - it's very clever. Michael loved his "Buffalo Bill" book and he and I have had no end of games of "Uncle Wiggley" he loves it. Elizabeth's book with the red window was admired by all and as far as the doll!! - my dear Mary, "Margaret-Ann" is really beautiful -

you should have seen Elizabeth gaze at her when she opened the parcel and the clothes are really beautiful - after Christmas lunch I helped Elizabeth try on the whole wardrobe. It really is a beautiful doll - there is not one in the English shops to beat it in looks size or anything - the hair is so lovely and does not get tangled like English dolls' hair. Elizabeth has a dolls bed which is just right for Margaret-Ann and each night in she goes in her warm nightdress. Elizabeth loved her so much that she

wrote you a letter with great effort as she has not been to school yet and does not know her ABC, but she told me what to say and I wrote it down and then she copied it out herself. I hope you got it - and Michael too - he, of course writes all on his own. You are an expert on dolls clothes - my goodness, I thought I was good, but the clothes you made are just perfect. I really can't thank you enough for the lovely parcel.

Mother came for Christmas – she came on Christmas Eve so that Gilbert, John, Peter and I could go to midnight mass. The youngest (M& E) hung up their stockings and we all did jolly well! On the 26th I gave the usual family tea (17 of us in all). David is trying to become an actor and has been studying at R.A.D.A. in London. I believe he is really rather good. My sister Billie and her husband were a bit disappointed when he threw up his Army career – especially after getting into Sandhurst. However, he seems much happier now, though at the time his step-father was very upset.

Willie, his wife and daughter are off to Penang at the end of March – they seem very glad.

My mother's eldest sister (Gladys) died last summer and Mother now lives in her small cottage in Ewhurst, Surrey – in the country – Mother is very happy but she prefers town life and I, who live in a town, hate crowds and like the country!

Schools in England are very complicated. Being a Roman Catholic, my boys go to an R.C. school – Bart was a very strict R.C. and I have kept to this to please him and because I have found it unwise to change one's religion. I myself have found it very hard to be an R.C.! However, I am wandering from the point. There are council schools – they are free and the very poor children go there – such as dustmen's sons and daughters – charwomen's children etc. But I have known quite nice people's children go (not that dustmen's children aren't nice, but you know what I mean – I'm not a snob!) but I find that children that do always get a cockney accent. Then there are the Grammar Schools where a small fee is paid. Then there are schools taken over by the "Board of Education" and they are free and only entered on scholarship. Then there are the Public Schools – they are THE schools to go to – the fees are pretty high – some higher *than others· My sons go to this class of school but mind you I don't pay the fees, the Ministry of Pensions and the R·A·F· Benevolent Fund are doing this for me because of Bart· You can get scholarships into them and I believe they have to take so many scholarships from grammar and council schools (I shall try to get Michael to take one) but I was lucky when I got John into the Oratory· The new headmaster was trying to make up the number at the school and so John got in without taking an entrance exam· Both Peter and Michael will have to take it· Now Peter and Michael are at another kind of school, a private school – it is run by a man and his wife and really I am pleased with it· They only take boys from 5 – 14· Of course there are night schools and Universities·*

Gilbert and I have been reading that book called "Flying Saucers have Landed" by George Adamski and D Lesily – it's most interesting and I can't help thinking there is something in it all· During the eclipse of the sun last summer, people in air craft saw strange things – I wonder what it all really is? · · · "

The next tenants that came to live in our flat were an old couple whom I liked but they didn't stay long. Then we got Barbara and Alan Rawlinson and Barbara's two daughters, Sue and Ann Greaves. Mother did miniatures of Barbara and one of the two

Ann and Sue

girls. They stayed for a few years and were good tenants. Mother gave Alan a fur hat and was amused (and slightly irritated) when she heard him tell someone: "Oh yes, I got this hat when I was out in Russia!" When they moved out to no 29 we took down the "petition" that separated some of the rooms on the middle floor from the rest of the house and had our whole house back.

From "Chessington Cottage", Worcester Park
9th December 1955

"· · · Sq/Ldr and Mrs W left and I now have a very nice, easy-going couple, with their two small girls aged 6 and 5 years (Barbara and Alan Rawlinson and Sue and Ann) · · ·
· · · Elizabeth was most interested in the photos· She is going to school now and can read quite well, only simple words but it is amazing how much she can read in her first term· For the first year she only goes from 9 am to 12:30 pm and it's rather a bother as you just get your housework done and half way to preparing lunch (tiffin) when you have to stop and dash off, catch a bus and meet her coming out of school·

The picture shows Mother and me on our way to the Royal Academy in London. The box Mother is carrying contains one of her miniatures of me.

Things have gone a bit better this year: I got a miniature I did of Elizabeth into the

146

Royal Academy, the tenants left, Peter passed his school entrance exam into the Oratory School and passed well.

Gilbert leaves school this term. He has joined the R·N·V·R· and goes up once a week to the H·M·S· President on the Thames in London. It's a cruiser moored by the Embankment with the Discovery and Chrysanthemum – all of which belong to the R·N·V·R· Gilbert wants to go into the diving branch of the R· Navy. I'm not too keen, but you can't stop a boy doing what he is dead keen on. Gilbert's call up for National Service comes in March or it may be September now as there has been an alteration – we are waiting to hear. · · · "

She continued to do miniatures. Having done one of Barbara and one of Sue and Ann she had Dulcie pose and painted her. These were exhibited at The Society of Miniaturists.

Although she tried to paint Bart posthumously she was never satisfied and the best are a pencil drawing and a caricature.

She was annoyed when, at The Oratory, Peter's poor English report was obviously not correct since Peter was good at English. She said the teacher was probably thinking of

John, whose strengths were always Maths and Science. Peter told her that during the cricket season the teacher, Mr Hobson, spent all his time on the pitch and not with his English classes. I assume that her complaint was properly dealt with because she kept the boys at the school and Michael followed them there.

To Mary from *"Chessington Cottage"*, Worcester Park
29ᵗʰ April 1956

". . . Elizabeth is now going to school full day from 9 o'clock until 3:30 pm. She has her lunch at school. The boys have just gone back to boarding school – the last day at home is always gloomy!! If only I had a car it wouldn't be so bad . . .

I'm keeping busy – doing my own garden (almost ½ an acre) I find it does me good to get out of the house – though when one is in the garden the time just flies by and you work longer and harder then you meant to and get terribly tired. I love it!

. . . Gilbert goes into the Navy in September. He goes for two weeks on a course in July with the Navy. At the moment he is filling in time with an odd job working for Carters the seed people. Not very exciting but I think it's made him stand on his own feet and he has quite liked it and been able to save quite a bit. John took a job this holidays and made over £8 in two weeks.

I've got a miniature of Elizabeth into the Royal Academy again this year. This time it is a side view and really sweeter than last year.

The private view is next Friday 4th.
Love to you and the children
        Zou Zou."

Every so often a gypsy would come to sell clothes pegs or "cross our palms with silver". Mother treated her as she would any visitor, from the Pope down to a tramp. One day she invited the old woman in for a cup of tea. The gypsy poured her tea carefully from the cup into the saucer and blew on it to cool it before drinking it loudly from the saucer. I watched in amazement and wondered if I should do the same. Mother, however, just continued to chatting to the woman and obviously didn't notice.

In 1949 the law regarding a man's death intestate said that all his goods should be put in trust for his surviving children and they would inherit their share at majority (the age of 21). The mother did not inherit anything except the right to bring up the children and live in their house. Both Mother and Aunt Agnes were appointed as trustees. This meant that for any major decision Agnes would have to agree. Later, when Mother wanted to pay off the mortgage with a no-interest loan from the RAF Benevolent Fund, Agnes initially refused to agree, causing a lot of ill-feeling. Eventually she reluctantly agreed.

The RAF Benevolent Fund was always very helpful. They sorted out the widow's pension and over the years were often able to assist when times were particularly hard. The pension was paid quarterly on September, December, March and June 10th. There was also a Children's Pension that arrived six-monthly on the 21st April and October. It was very difficult to make ends meet. Always by the end of the quarter there were red bills waiting to be paid. Sometimes she would buy something more expensive at the end of the quarter, paying for it from the next instalment of pension – something new always cheered her up when money was a particular worry. In this way we gradually acquired luxuries such as a Hoover, a washing machine, a fridge and a TV. I remember that when I went to university and got the full grant of about £450 for the year, I was amazed because it was almost the same amount as Mother's pension.

In 1956 when Willie returned to England he looked very much better than he had for some time. Within a few weeks there was another terrible shock; Mother wrote to Mary:

Willie Howell loved the RAF. The left-hand picture was used in a cigarette advert.

"Chessington Cottage", Worcester Park
29th September 1956

"Dearest Mary,
*   I'm afraid this is going to be a sad letter as we have lost Willie now.*
It came as a terrible shock as he and his wife and daughter only arrived
home from Singapore early this month. We've not seen Willie looking so
well since his accident in 1949. He'd put on weight and looked awfully
well. On arriving he stayed with my sister, Dulcie, and then went down to
stay at Gwen's mother for a short holiday and then Gwen went to stay
with a friend, while Willie was sent to West Raynham R·A·F· station
(where Bart was in command during the Battle of Britain) Willie shared
a room with and officer called Valentine whom he'd known before. He and
Valentine got up last Sunday morning – had breakfast and then went out
to Valentine's car – he asked Willie to give it a push – which W· did and

then he opened the door for W. to get in the car. He said Willie just stood there and said: "I really must give up smoking!" He took 3 deep breaths and then fell. Valentine jumped out of the car and got two orderlies to pick Willie up and carry him into the guards' room – they thought he had fainted and called the M.O. Valentine had to go but he came back in 20 minutes and you can imagine how he felt when told my brother was dead. The M.O. said he had died before he fell as he made no attempt to save his fall. They say it was thrombosis, but they had a post-mortem. We haven't yet heard the result. They say it must be the result of the bad crash in 1949. Willie was cremated yesterday, my birthday – so it was a very sad one. His wife is taking it very well – today she goes down to her mother's – Georgina is the one I'm really worried about as she worshipped the ground her father walked on – she is 14 years old so a nice age for her mother to have around.

Now for more happy events: My son Gilbert has been called up into the Royal Navy. He has had a fortnight in barracks at Portsmouth and today I had a card to say he was now on H.M.S. Vanguard. I do not know if it is home fleet or whether he will be going abroad. I am hoping he will make the Navy his career – he seems to love it and seems happy from his letters. John has passed his G.C.E. in Elementary and Additional Maths and I am in the midst of trying to get him into an electronics and radar firm here as an apprentice, which may mean him leaving school this term.

Well, Mary dear, I thought you would like to know about Willie as you knew him so well in Kobe – it's a terrible shock to us all. Mother is taking it well – though you see a change in her, as she keeps asking the same question again just after you've given her the answer – I expect that is caused by the shock and you know she is 70 years old though she doesn't look it. . . ."

Georgina wrote: "When it comes to my father's death, I didn't know the name of the man whose car he fatally helped to push. But there is something wrong in this letter. My mother and I did not come home with my father from Malaya. He went on ahead of us to find somewhere for us to live. I wrote to him on his arrival in England – I can't remember *where I wrote from – and in fact we were still in transit when he died. On our arrival we were met by some old friends from Driffield, the Barbers, who took us to their home telling us my father was waiting for us there. When we got there I was left in a room with a lot of books and they told my mother that Bill (as we called him) was dead. Then we went to Gwen's mother in Malvern where I stayed while my mother struggled to find a flat in London where we could afford to live."*

Willie, by Zou Zou.

Our family had only two holidays away from Worcester Park together. We had a few days one year staying in Hove at Joyce Bartholomew's house while she and our cousins were away. I think Mother took Michael and me on the train while the older boys went by bicycle. We took our new kitten with us. The weather wasn't too wonderful with huge waves crashing on the beach on one of the days.

It was quite normal for children to wear their school coats and blazers during the holidays because they were the only warm coats they had.

This is in Brighton.

Miniatures: *"Billie Beaumont" (ex. RA 1938, 30 x 40mm);*

Self portrait – 1933 (75 x 55mm);

"Willie" (above)

"Michael aged 4" (ex.1952, 75 x 55mm); right

"Michael 1960" (75 x 55mm);

"John" - aged about 19 – in oils

Peter recalls our life in Worcester Park:

"Religiously, Mother insisted that we attend mass every Sunday but I never caught on to the fact that she NEVER did. Dad was a devout catholic and mother kept to his wishes that we should have a 'good catholic education'. On leaving school I stopped because I realised that there was more to religion than Catholicism and less religion and no conscience in Catholicism, just dogma. I think that the Jesuits did it for all three elder boys."

In fact I remember that she did go sometimes. On one occasion I had been slow (maybe naughty) and everyone left, including Mother, to go to mass at nine. I knew that there was a service at ten so I left the house on my own at ten (not remembering that it took a good twenty minutes to walk to St Matthias) and met the family coming up The Avenue. Was I really left on my own? No, I think the people in the flat had probably been asked to keep an eye on me. As for the boys and religion: I think Gilbert was the only one who tried to keep the faith going. I certainly did not want to be confirmed at the age of ten because I didn't believe it all and begged Mother to get me out of it. She wrote to the school and said that since I had been off school with a cold we didn't think I was really ready and it was postponed. When I got to the Ursuline at eleven there was no way out and I grudgingly was confirmed. Merrial Webb used to drag me to church regularly but I went for the company and the cycle ride rather than for the faith. I spent the rest of my school days as an undercover atheist.

Mother also liked a young priest who joined the parish, Father Ingleton. He visited us often, and I remember he came to lunch a few times when the boys were home – he must have been a little older than Gilbert. She liked him to visit because she was aware that we all questioned the Faith and she wanted to give God and Bart a chance to guide us back. She herself was driven away from Catholicism by Agnes and Mrs B's interpretation of it. She believed in God and in life after death but her God was generous and forgiving. Once she moved to Milford she tried all sorts of different religions: Quakers, Jehovah's Witness, Spiritualism included.

To Mary: *From "Chessington Cottage", Worcester Park*
15ᵗʰ February 1957

". . . Just after Christmas, I had workmen in to decorate 3 rooms - now I've had most rooms done - and there is only my bedroom and the hall left to do. I have done away with the box-room and made it into a nice bedroom for Gilbert and Michael. Peter and John have the other attic room. The first floor is the flat I let and on the ground floor is my drawing room, kitchen and dining room, my room and Elizabeth's room.

My room is large and I'm making it into a studio too. I've decided to take up miniature painting really seriously now that I have more time. I have just been elected a member of the Society of Miniaturists and am busy painting two miniatures of the children upstairs to send into their exhibition in March. I intend to join the Royal Society of Miniaturists too. I only hope to meet some artists this way, as I lost touch with all I knew and of course my best friend died in the war.

I felt I must do something or go round the bend! People nowadays seem so unkind and unfriendly - no time for anyone but themselves - and most women go out to work and leave their husbands flat and their children too. I can't understand it. It all seems so unfair. My neighbours on one side - a doctor and his wife and 3 children are not ideal!!! Sometimes she is all over you and the next she passes you by as if she hasn't seen you! - it depends on her mood, so I just take her as her mood comes! And I don't worry overmuch now, but at first it was a bit of a problem. She sails past me each day in her car taking her child to school and I walking with Elizabeth to catch a bus. At first these things hurt a bit, but now it doesn't. I wave and she hoots her horn at me as she passes and if she doesn't I don't wave! They have rather unruly children - 2 boys and a girl. The boys are 10 and 11 yrs old and friends of my Michael's but I'm getting rather worried as they seem to give their sons most dangerous things to play with - I removed the most dangerous catapult from Michael which one of these boys had asked him to look after (you can be taken before the juvenile court in England for having one) Then several times last holidays the elder boy asked if he could get his arrow back which had come over by my back door – You can imagine my horror when I found these boys had been given bows and arrows – real archery sets with nice sharp brass ends to the arrows and these things had been landing by my back door! My tenant, Alan Rawlinson, says if any more come over he will complain to Dr Bowen (their father). My nice neighbours left and sold their house to some people called Mr and Mrs Tucker – they seem quite nice – but I must say I'm not keen on north-country people they seem to be all out for "brass" as they call money!!

Since Willie's death, Mother seems to have cracked up. She is all right but very quiet and gets tired easily. She is still with my sister, Billie, and I think she will stay as I don't think she is strong enough to live on her own again.

Gilbert seems to be enjoying his time in the Navy – he is turning into such a nice young man – though I say it myself! John will be leaving school this summer term and going in for electronics.

Peter is going to be nice looking – he is growing fast now, I think he is 5ft 11 inches and looks more because he is so slim – once he fills out he will be smashing! He is only 15 ½ yrs old.

My hair is very grey now. I do it in a bun fairly high up – everyone says it looks nice. . ."

She grew her hair and started to wear it in a bun around 1956. I remember when she first put it up, she asked me what I thought and I said I didn't like it because she looked different. I'm glad to say she ignored my advice. It made looking after her hair easier. She said that a "perm" never lasted more than a day because her hair was so fine. I remember her warming iron curling-tongs on the gas stove, testing their heat on newspaper (it mustn't singe the paper) and curling the wisps of hair that invariably escaped around her face.

Then there was the time in 1957 when she went to Nelson Hospital to have an operation on her varicose veins. Granada (the pet name given to my grandmother, Gwen Howell, by Graham Duncombe) came to help at Worcester Park but John ended up doing most of the cooking because he was more capable than she was. Granada took me to see Mother in hospital. We marched up the ward together pursued by a nurse: "Children aren't allowed in the hospital wards," she told my grandmother. "Nonsense! Seeing Elizabeth is the one thing that will cheer my daughter up and make her well again!" So they put us in the corridor and brought Mother to us in a wheelchair. I remember that she spoke so quietly and how odd it was to see her weak and inactive.

To Mary: *From "Chessington Cottage", Worcester Park*
30ᵗʰ November 1957

· · · I had to go and see a specialist about my wretched leg which has been giving me quite a bit of pain – he advised an operation· I went into hospital on 26ᵗʰ Oct and had the op on 28ᵗʰ was 3 weeks in hospital and came out just two weeks ago· Mother is here helping· I'm not too good getting about yet, a bit wobbly – can't do shopping but will try next week, if I can· The operation was for varicose veins, this time they did the thing properly and took the veins out – cutting my leg from the knee down to the ankle!! So it was quite an operation – I was told it was a major one, is it? – anyway it's the new method·

John has now left school and is working for Decca – he is an apprentice at the moment he is being sent round the factories from one department to the other and then in a month or two he will start work properly – he is going in for radar and electronics·

Gilbert is still on H·M·S· Bulwark, an aircraft carrier – he's been all round England or rather Britain and Ireland and up past Norway towards

Iceland on NATO trials – says he may be home soon. He has been instructing some officers in diving. This is what he adores doing. I can't imagine why! He passed the R·N· shallow water diving test, which is an 8-week course and very tough out of twelve taking the course only 4 passed. . . "

From "Chessington Cottage", Worcester Park
10th January 1958
" · · · Christmas was rather quiet this year, somehow I didn't seem to get the real Christmas feeling – lots of people tell me they didn't either. Anyway we were all together – Gilbert managed to get Christmas and New Year this time; he went back on the 2nd. Last time he wrote he had just been re-stationed from H·M·S· Bulwark to H·M·S· Victorious. He was furious because he was looking forward to a trip abroad and H·M·S· Bulwark sails to Jamaica, Trinidad, Canada, Gibraltar and Hong Kong – in fact all the places Gilbert is longing to see.
· · · (your friends) called on me. They came without warning. I'd just spent the day gardening and had just come into the house, I was about to wash when they arrived, so I didn't look my best!! However, she was very nice and the little boy was full of beans · · · It was very nice to talk to someone who knew you.

I got so fed up with everybody here I found out the fare to and back from America – only to find it would cost £200 without extras, so I guess I'll have to stay fed up! I don't know what's wrong with everyone these days – the luckiest people moan and groan more than anyone else. My sister Billie being one of these! And Mother's always saying "Poor Billie" this and that – Poor Billie my foot! She has everything to make her happy – except her son is a bit trying and never sticks to a job – but that's her fault half the time. Then Mother (who lives with Billie) – she had a dear little cottage of her own, but no, she hated it and hated living in the country and so she goes and lives with Billie and the cottage is sold and the money for it split up between Mother and her two sisters (it was according to Gladys's will when she died that Mother had the cottage as long as she lived or wanted it·) Then Mother is always complaining about herself being a widow and myself too· The difference in our ages never occurs to her – I was only 37 and she was 68 when we became widows – she had 50 years with my father; I had 14 and 6 of those Bart and I were parted during the war – so really I only had 8 years· She just doesn't realise how lucky she was at my age when she was having a gay old time – She must have been 39 or 40 when we were in Kobe (at the date of this letter Zou is 46) Think of that!

To turn up at Billie's without an invitation is almost an unforgivable sin! And I'll tell you this, she has only come to see me ONCE since Bart died without being invited, and when invited she and her husband turn up just in time for lunch and then dash off just afterwards – he to go to a rugger match and she goes to his sister's·   That's why I'm fed up·

Dulcie calls quite often and is sweet, but has a husband whom I think is rather selfish – however, they are both happy and that is what matters – Anyway this year my New Year's resolution is not to ask Billie here and see if I see her at all!!? It's funny she should be so happy·   I hope you don't mind my blowing my top to you – it helps a bit· I don't want anyone to be sorry for me – but one does get lonely sometimes and I did help Billie quite a lot when her first marriage went on the rocks – Oh well, enough of that·
I went to a party last night – the first in a year! It was quite nice – got a commission to paint 2 children's miniatures, so that's something nice to do·
I've got nice neighbours one side but I told you about the other – she is still very difficult – so I keep well away – even the children do too·
A black kitten (half grown) walked into our house last night and is still here – so that's lucky – maybe 1958 will be a nice and happier year·
I was told by an old lady last night at the party that I looked really lovely

– so that was a nice thing to happen. It was your dress and stockings too!

　　Well Mary, I hope I haven't depressed you – count your blessings – I suppose I have some too – my health, my nice sons, a nice home and garden – in fact I'm really very happy, except I would like to be taken out a bit – sometimes one gets very lonely.

　　My leg is so much better and once the scar turns white I don't think it will show.

　　Lots of love, Zou Zou"

From "Chessington Cottage", Worcester Park
1ˢᵗ July 1958
" · · · I am feeling much better now – was very down after my operation – I don't know why.

　　The children are all fine.

　　I am hoping to make this house back into a house soon. Now that the boys are older it's very cramped in this flat, so I've asked the people to go and they are looking for a house. · · ·"

From "Chessington Cottage", Worcester Park
29ᵗʰ July 1958
" · · · I have just bought a second hand car for John. It's an Austin and he has taken Peter, Elizabeth and Michael to the sea for the day.

Gilbert comes home tomorrow and I am trying to cope with unpacking Peter's and Michael's trunks and doing their washing. It's a nice windy day for drying.

I was wondering if you could help me try to contact an old friend of mine – he is an Austrian (but may have become an American citizen) His name is HANS SEMMLER and is manager of a hotel in New York – he would only be in the really good class of hotel – I have a hunch that he is in N.Y. He had the wander lust so he may be anywhere – but is it possible to find out if he is in New York? He was one of the finest men I ever met. I thought I'd ask you · · · I would also like to try and contact Roxy Kovalski (now Kemp) I find old friends are best. I don't like the average English woman. They seem to be just out for all the gossip they can get and if they can't get it they make up. · · ·

My people upstairs go soon. I hope I will be able to manage without the rent – bit worried about it as this house takes a bit of keeping up as it is over 100 years old.! Ah well! I must now get on with the ironing. · · ."

Mother also tried to trace Sinclair – a friend from her student days – with no success.

From "Chessington Cottage", Worcester Park
18th October 1958

"Dearest Mary,
It was nice of you to go to all that trouble to find Hans Semmler. I wrote to the address you gave me (2230 79th Street NY) but my letter was returned today unopened, so he must have left or WHAT? You'd think if he'd been there and left, the people would readdress it. I just can't understand it.

Hans was an Austrian, came from Vienna – he would be about 59 or 60 years old now job: manager of a Hotel. In England foreigners have to report to the police every so often. Would he therefore have to report to the N.Y. police? could I get in touch with him that way?? I think his name may have been Heinz – it rang a bell when I saw it written – though I always called him Hans. He was badly wounded in World War I – had a plate in his nose as the bones were smashed to bits. I wish I could trace him if he is still alive.

· · · Yes, Gilbert has signed on in the Navy and he begins his diving course on Monday 20th October. It is a very stiff one and 90% fail. He's so keen I <u>do</u> hope he will make it.   John has passed his first lot of exams in maths and electronics, also his driving test – he has an Austin 7 car. Funny how boys are so lazy with lessons and girls take them seriously – evidently American boys are the same! Elizabeth now reads anything even the newspaper!!! Long words too – it amazes me. Michael is doing quite well. He is 11 years old in a class with boys of 12 and 13. They say he could beat the lot if he wished but he is lazy. · · ·"

From "Chessington Cottage", Worcester Park
26th February 1959

" · · · Yes, I often see Willie's wife and Daughter. They stayed with me for Christmas and I am having Gina for 3 weeks at Easter while Gwen goes out to stay with friends in Ankara. Gwen is very nice and I like her and I think she is fond of me too. They have a flat in London and Worcester Park is only 20 minutes in a train to London. Gwen is one of those people who is never put out – though she's stayed with me heaps of times before and after her marriage to my brother – never once has she asked me to stay with them – not even after Bart's death and they were stationed so near where my boys went to boarding school. · · · Billie blames her for us not seeing Willie very much. But · · I think Willie was to blame too. I'm certainly angry with him for not seeing my mother and father more often. My mother adored him and he could do no wrong in her eyes. · · · Gwen seems more thoughtful now – writes to my mother every week and Gina is dressed nicely too. Anyway, for all her faults, I like Gwen – I guess we all have our bad points!! · · ·"

Washing day was usually weekly on Monday and our washing machine was an electric tub into which you put hot water and detergent and it had an electric motor to agitate the load. On top there was a mangle. Mother used to mangle the soapy clothes into the bath which contained clean rinsing water and then mangle them back before hanging them out on the line across the yard by the scullery. The job took a long time and so we tended to wear the same clothes for several days to keep the washing to a minimum. At some point in the sixties the old machine was replaced by a Hoovermatic Twin-tub – a really modern invention.

Generally Zou Zou was very frugal. She rarely bought new clothes and we children often got hand-me-downs from neighbours and friends. Compared to my own children and those nowadays, I had very few clothes – maybe only one or two changes of clothes apart from my school uniform. New clothes were part of Christmas or birthdays.

There were no charity shops then to buy quality used clothes so it could be difficult, but Mother always managed to dress well.   When jeans became available in the fifties, partly because of the advent of the "teenager" and the "teddy-boy", Mother bought jeans for the boys to wear during the holidays. She said they were wonderful; at last boys had tough trousers which would take rough wear and would wash well. She said that some people frowned on them saying only the lowest class of boy would wear them!

She tried to save for the future and always bought her National Insurance stamps. In those days you had a card and literally bought special stamps at the post office to stick on it. She kept it up and at 60 got a full State Pension.

We were very lucky to have a house of our own which grew in value. The upkeep was costly and we had to have the roof and gutters repaired during the 50's.

Bart had built a garage at the side of the house. It was a wooden frame with flat asbestos sheeting for the roof and walls. Mother said that sometime later a council official called to say it had no planning permission. He told her that you could go to prison for putting up a building unlawfully. Mother said, "Well that would be a welcome holiday for me; you will look after the children won't you?" She said he went away and she heard no more about it.

Christmas was always very special. Mother loved rich decorations, and we always had a real tree which was decorated with all sorts of colourful things, many of them brought out year after year. There were electric coloured lights. She always finished the tree off with cotton wool along each branch, with maybe a sprinkling of glitter dust – this looked like real snow. The streamers that went from the central ceiling light to the corners of the room had threads of silver tinsel hung on each joint giving the room a feeling of icicles hanging down in a cave. A crib was set up on a shelf or near the tree and this had all the Holy Family, shepherds, angels and kings as well as animals and a small mirror as a pond with a little swan. Cotton wool again made snow and a lantern glowed in the stable/cave. The baby was added last thing on Christmas Eve. The kings only arrived at the manger on the Epiphany, having been very close by, and as soon as they got there the decorations were taken down. The preparation for Christmas took a lot of time and often was quite stressful, but the result was magical.

Each of us would choose a chair or part of the sofa on Christmas Eve and we would hang our stocking there. In the morning each place would be filled with presents, the fire would be lit and then we would open everything. As the older boys grew they took to giving each other a £1 note for Christmas, except, because it was agreed, the actual pound note didn't have to exist at all but they always warmly thanked each other. If anyone was slow to rise on Christmas morning, Mother would put one of our 78s on the gramophone (record player) – a chorus from J. S. Bach – Wachet Auf.

We often had guests at Christmas – Granada, Gwen and Georgina – in 1955 we probably had Willie, Dulcie, Geoff, Billie, Graham and David, and Agnes and Grandma Bartholomew. The main meal was always turkey with stuffing, gravy, roast potatoes, cabbage (she didn't like sprouts) carrots, bread sauce and some Woodpecker Cider for all of us to drink. I think you could buy that down at Trimmers shop at the bottom of the road and then take the bottles back after Christmas to claim a few pence back. The Christmas pudding was sometimes made by Mrs B. It was in a bowl which had to be wrapped and tied in a cloth and steamed or cooked in the pressure cooker. We had sweet white sauce with it. In the afternoon there would be cold-meat sandwiches, mince pies and Christmas cake. Agnes and Mrs B. would come to tea and usually a sherry too – "Steady, Mother!" says Agnes.

Around 1960 her Aunt Iva and Granada were invited by an old friend to holiday in Switzerland. Van Smith ran a hotel in Engelburg and wanted to show them around. They asked Zou Zou to accompany them as she was younger and would be a help to them and they felt it would be good for her health. They went by boat and then train. Mother loved the place but hated the ferry as she got seasick. She had not been abroad since 1949.

She brought back a cuckoo whistle and a little clock for Michael and a musical box for me, which confusingly played the Swedish Rhapsody.

Zou Zou
and
Aunt Iva
on
Lake
Lucerne

1960-ish

I remember in August 1961 being called in from the garden by my mother, who was in a tearful state. She told Michael and me that our cousin David had died. The shock was such that I almost laughed. David was a nice young man of 27. When I had stayed at Shamley Green with Billie and Graham once, David had spent some time with me while the adults downstairs had a cocktail party in honour of Granada's birthday. We played hangman and consequences and we took it in turn to change each other's scribbles into pictures. I remember clearly my scribble being turned into a picture of a suffragette chained in a barrel.

He wrote poems and a play and made contacts with the RSC and John Whiting[1]. He moved to Oxford but became very depressed about his lack of success and in August 1961 he phoned his mother, Billie, to tell her he intended to end it all. Billie rushed to Oxford but arrived to find him collapsed after taking sleeping pills. He never regained consciousness and Billie never got over her grief.

---

[1] British dramatist John Whiting (1917-1963) had a peculiar career in the English-language theatre. After writing *A Penny for a Song*, *Saint's Day* and *Marching Song*, which enjoyed brief runs in the West End and were greeted with considerable confusion if not contempt in the early 1950s, he wrote nothing for the theatre between 1954 and 1960, though he did contribute criticism and reviews to publications such as *London Magazine*. Whiting returned to the theatre in 1960; of his major work he completed only *The Devils* before dying of cancer three years later at the age of 45. Upon his death, actress Peggy Ashcroft said, "We have lost one of our finest dramatists but also a major critic."

David Stuart Duncombe (Thunder) (1934 - 1961)

From *"Chessington Cottage"*, *Worcester Park*
10ᵗʰ December 1962

"· · · *Gilbert is in Singapore for two years so there will be only the five of us and my mother here for Christmas·*

I enclose a cutting from the local paper (Surrey Comet Dec· 8ᵗʰ 1962) about Peter which I hope will interest you· Michael Collier of Micol Productions was heard to say "They're great!" He has signed Peter's group and their first record comes out on Decca (England) and Liberty (USA)· They cut it next week· When "The Escorts" went up for their audition they sang one of Peter's own numbers· George Cooper (an agent) stopped them and said "I know that number· I've just picked it out of some new ones sent me; it's by Peter Bartholomew," and of course the group laughed and said "Well, this is Peter" So maybe that will be on one side of the record· I don't know if you like this sort of music· Personally I like all music from Beethoven to jazz and Rock 'n Roll too· Anyway if you have any friends over there that like it, do introduce them to "the Escorts" on "Liberty" records·

The Escorts became the Overlanders - initially with just three members: Peter, Laurie Mason and Paul Arnold Friswell.

Peter had been in a group ever since school where "Bart and his Bashers" had provided entertainment. "Peter of The Archangels" is immortalised in another of Mother's miniatures which was exhibited at The Royal Society of Miniature Painters Sculptors & Gravers 63rd exhibition in 1961.

The house at Worcester Park, of course, had no central heating. There were fireplaces in all the downstairs rooms. We usually lit the coal fire in the drawing room and then a gas fire was installed in the study. I remember a small black stove in the kitchen which ran on coke and could be used to boil a kettle and to give some heat. We had a gas cooker in the scullery. The stove was replaced in the early 1950s by a Rayburn which also heated our water and was a huge improvement. Its heat helped dry the clothes on the airer that hung from the ceiling in front of it.

Mother said she hated cooking. She had had to learn to cook during the war using dried egg and "klim" (dried milk) and making little go a long way. Then she had to learn all over again when at last you could get good ingredients again. She had a sweet tooth and missed cakes and sweets during the war. She always loved butter and real milk. They hadn't had cows' milk in China and after the war she found she could get "gold top" milk – Channel Islands milk, which was extra creamy – a luxury she felt was worth the extra.

During the 1950's, when housework in such a large house was much more labour intensive and when she had few of the mod-cons that came in the '60s, she did employ some help. Mrs Cook and then Mrs Garrity used to come for a few hours to help with the housework. Mother enjoyed using the Hoover Junior on the carpets – she used it almost every day and when we were slow to get up she would hoover to wake us up!

For the garden she enlisted the help of Mr Courtney. He liked the children and terrified Mother once when, in order to entertain them he demonstrated "fire-breathing". He took a small mouthful of spirit and then blew it out over a flame which ignited it and made a fireball. She was frightened they might try it themselves and either swallow methylated spirit or burn themselves badly.

Courtney also worked at Elliot and James' shop on Central Road, Worcester Park, which sold bicycles, toy soldiers and figures and Hornby trains, and fireworks in November. The handlebar had broken off our tricycle and I could steer it only by holding the hooked top of the stem. Mother took it to the shop and they welded the handlebar back on. I remember going out into their back yard to look for it but I couldn't find it among the bikes that were there until it was pointed out. Mother once was passing the shop when he called her in to show her a fox that was in their back yard. She said it had almost grey fur and was beautiful. It managed to jump back onto the wall and get away. I was very envious of her seeing a fox – my favourite wild animal and one that I had only seen in books.

We kept the milk in the larder and the meat under a meat-safe – a wire dome which kept the flies off. The larder had a window that was permanently open but covered by a perforated zinc sheet. I remember when in the late 50's we got our first refrigerator. This was also an expensive luxury. The first television we had was a large piece of furniture about three feet tall and fifteen inches square with a grey screen a foot wide. It was second-hand but she knew that would be cheaper in the long run than renting a TV as many people did in those days. We could view the BBC on it. Mother said she got it so that we wouldn't spend so much time watching the Bowens' TV next door.

Like a lot of families we enjoyed listening to the radio – "Music While You Work", "Family Favourites", "Children's Choice", "Have a Go", "Billy Cotton Band Show", "The Archers", "Hancock's Half-Hour" and so on. Peter remembers: *At Worcester Park we used to listen to the "Goon Show" on the Radio-Gram. We all tried to imitate the varied voices of the goons, and mother would come out with 'I've been bonced!' which had us amused because the goons never said that."*

Programmes that gave her a lot of enjoyment were the plays on the radio and the music on the Light Programme. She always had "Housewives Choice" on in the morning and a song that would stop her in her tracks was Kathleen Ferrier singing "What is life to be without you; what is life if thou art dead?" – from Gluck's "Orpheus and Eurydice". She identified with Orpheus' loss of his beloved.

She enjoyed music and used to play "Fur Elise" on the piano as well as a piece written by Granada called "Joy and Sorrow". She had a newish upright piano on which I started to learn to play. Then we took Granada's rosewood upright which had a much lighter action and a lovely tone so Mother sold the small one. A couple of visits to the antiques auction house in Cheam resulted in us owning two player-pianolas and some scrolls. These she loved because, at last, she could play Beethoven and Chopin quickly and correctly.

We had lots of musical instruments in the house as I grew up. Some had belonged to my father. There was a banjo, a violin, bagpipes and an accordion, a ukulele, a large bass drum, piano and later guitars as well. I was amazed when I was thirteen or fourteen and my mother picked up the ukulele and strummed it and sang a song – I had no idea she knew how to play it! She was always able to sing quietly along to songs of the twenties, thirties and forties. She especially liked songs that were witty and happy. She had been a fan of the "Whispering Baritone" (Jack Smith) and of Charlie Kunz, Flannigan and Allan and George Formby. She loved 1930s and '40s songs and referred to them as jazz, but oddly she never understood the real jazz of the age; she said Willie could sit down at a piano and improvise jazzed-up music. She didn't like it because it hid the tune for her and sounded un-melodious.

She could whistle quite sweetly and sing in tune although she had a very quiet voice. She always said she could whistle (very unladylike) better than she could sing. I remember many songs that were used to entertain me as a small child. She would sing to me as she put me to bed. Her favourites: "A Froggie would a-wooing go", "It Ain't Gonna Rain No More, No More", "Horsey, Horsey, Don't You Stop", "The Owl and the Pussy Cat", "Tiny Man", "Felix kept on Walking", "Mairzy Dotes an' Dozy Dotes". Because she listened daily to the Light Programme and then to Radio 1, she got to enjoy the pop music of the late '50s and the 1960s especially when Peter became a pop singer. She bought a number of 45s, preferring happy songs and love songs of which there were many.

She was also fond of reading. She recommended books like "White Fang" (Jack London), "The Citadel" (A.J.Cronin), "The Good Earth" (Pearl Buck), and "The Well of Loneliness" (Radclyffe Hall) as well as Dickens.

In 1963 Isobel Curry, Ursula's elder sister, was involved in the running of the Women's Institute and commissioned mother to do simple illustrations for a small pamphlet of baking recipes they were compiling. The colours were limited to two for the cover and one for inside. Bread and cakes had to be a brown and she said periwinkle blue was a good addition for the cover.

I don't know how much she earnt from this - not a lot I think - and she is not credited in it.

As I remember my childhood, I recall my mother as warm and loving and totally dependable. However, should you be naughty she could be very firm. When she was upset or angry, I learnt to lose myself in the garden or upstairs and be quiet for a long while until I was sure she had recovered (or forgiven me!). She was often stressed by fears over money and by loneliness and she would suffer bad headaches. She said once that on those occasions it was always John who would return from playing in the garden to ask "Are you better, Mummy?" The rest of us took it more in our stride as a normal, temporary need to be quieter.

She loved the garden and worked hard to keep it pretty. Whenever a visitor came there would be talk of old times, news of the present, lunch or tea and cakes, and then an obligatory tour of the garden. Mother would carry a trowel and dig up bits of plants people admired so that they could propagate them in their own gardens.

She would happily swat a wasp or fly. She often said "Zola!" ("Go away") to a fly and very often it seemed to understand. If one of the boys was around they would have to deal with any large house spiders which always scared her. Otherwise she was fond of animals. She loved to see the hedgehog and put out food for it.

We had plenty of pets while at Chessington Cottage. We had a tortoise, rabbits, guinea pigs, hamsters, fish, terrapins, mice and birds and we had a succession of cats several of which were the offspring of Minnie who lived a few houses down the road with Mrs Kent.

We bought "Jade of Roke" when I was seven in 1957. We called her Pao Pei (precious one) – a name chosen from Pearl Buck's book: "The Chinese Children Next Door". Mother didn't really like other people's dogs but she said they always would come and lie at her feet when she visited any house that had one.

Pao Pei was a Pekinese and therefore not a real dog. Mother thought the puppy might be able to sleep in her room but found the dog snored so loudly that it was impossible so after the first night Pao Pei had her bed in the kitchen.

Once, when we drove the Austin 7 to Banbury to visit Michael in school, we drove out into the countryside and the car broke down. We were near a farm building and John went for help. The farmer gladly assisted John while the rest of us had a cup of tea in the farmhouse. The woman there told her little boy to take us outside to see the bantams. I had no idea what a "bantam" was and imagined rabbits. They turned out to be small chickens. When we admired them the woman went to get a box and gave us two half-grown chicks. At home we built a run for them and, since they turned out to be a cock and a hen, we soon had a small flock.

They were kept on a bit of ground at the back of the garden beyond the bonfire patch. They were good layers and we had lots of small eggs.

On one occasion the birds escaped and it took us a long time to capture them all because they are light and can fly quite well compared to standard chickens. They sat on the top of the rose poles – about eight feet up - and watched us.

Occasionally the eggs stopped for a several days and we discovered that someone was climbing into the garden and taking them. Mother was very angry and thought it was probably the Bowen boys next door. She hard-boiled one egg and took another one and punctured it and put both back in the nest boxes when she felt sure the second one was bad. Both these eggs disappeared without trace, much to Mother's satisfaction.

Mother's favourite pets were her birds; she loved the colours of the foreign finches and parrots, the songs of the canaries and the intelligence of the starlings and mynahs. She kept birds up until the late 1970s.

A young man who was leaving to go to university to study veterinary science gave us a rabbit and a Lesser Indian Hill Mynah called Fella. They moved house with us to Milford.

In the '50s she bought a pair of red-eared waxbills and kept them in a fairly small bird cage. In the summer we would put them and the canary outside to enjoy the sunshine and the wild birdsong. One day I thought I'd like to give them something and I opened the cage door and one escaped. Mother put out a separate cage beside the occupied one, with seed in it and an open door which could be quickly closed. A little later we saw a bird in the cage and shut the door. We had caught *two* red-eared waxbills! Where the second one had come from we never knew.

There were grey squirrels at Worcester Park. In about 1954 a baby squirrel appeared in the garden. He was too young to feed himself but seemed to have no parents looking after him. Some trees had been felled up near the library in Shadbolt Park and we decided that the adults had probably been killed. Mother crept out of the back door and caught the baby squirrel under a meat-safe mesh dome (normally used to cover a joint in the larder to keep flies off).

We used a wooden packing case (about 6x3x3 feet) and chicken wire to make a cage for him and called him Twinkleberry after Squirrel Nutkin's well-behaved brother. The poor thing couldn't even crack open peanuts at first so we gave him bread and milk and shelled nuts. His staple food soon became hazelnuts and acorns (of which we had a good supply in season). At the side of the house was a larger wooden packing case (6x5x3 feet or so) which had been made into a Wendy-house with a door and window. Outside this was a sandpit. Mother bought some wood and chicken wire and Courtney, who came to help with the gardening once a week, built a cage around the Wendy-house and the sandpit. Branches and shelves were added as well as a box of oak leaves inside the house. Twinks was put in this cage and lived there for several years until another squirrel tempted him to bite through the wire and escape. Then we built a second cage for him at the top of the garden from which he ventured daily and then later left altogether to live in the trees with the other squirrels. He was our pet for ten years – eventually living free. He was still alive when we left Worcester Park in 1964 and Mrs Macintosh down the road knew Twinks and continued to feed him and his friends for some time after we left. She wrote the story of "Twinks" and illustrated it but it has mostly been lost.

He kindly sent me a card on my 5th birthday.

Mother liked to see the animals housed with a lot of space. She would use whatever wood was available and buy chicken wire and staples. There were many occasions when we built cages and runs for various creatures. One of the boys coined the term "Miracles with Sticks" to describe our cages.

Other wild animals became our pets. During the autumn, field mice would come into the house to live in the larder. John made a cage trap and we caught them and put them in a large tank cage that we built on the clay mound by the cherry tree. We fed them until spring when we released them back into the wild. Mother also rescued a hedgehog from the road and kept it until it had recovered.

Once she was walking up the road from shopping when a slow-worm slid into the roadway. She thought it would be run over so she picked it up and put it in her handbag and took it home to release it in our back garden.

She was somewhat naïve and trusting but could be unforgiving if someone (such as Mrs Bowen our neighbour) upset her. She was often envious of people who had more than her especially if they had no money worries. She said more than once when hearing of a man and his wife who were unhappy together: "Why did God take Bart, when he could have taken that man instead?" She was especially upset by the insensitivity and thoughtlessness she sometimes found in people around her who were not widowed and who had fewer worries than her.

She considered herself upper-middle-class, but she was friends with many down-to-earth people and detested self-important people and snobs. She often felt out of touch and a foreigner in her own land. Sometimes her rather uneven, sketchy education and her unusual childhood let her down. Her spelling and sometimes her grasp of politics, maths and science was not very good. However, this made her extraordinarily proud of the achievements of her children.

During the 1960s there was a push for new houses close to London and a number of the old places on The Avenue were seeking planning permission. Dr Dene next-door-but-one sold his house and land for a close of houses which later bore his name. The big, red brick, Victorian house opposite ours then had builders move into its large, neglected garden to start on a big estate there (finally demolishing the old house as well).   Our neighbour, Dr Bowen, built a new house in his back garden that linked to the end of Dene Close overlooking our back garden. In her letter to Mary she says:

(10th December 1962)

"I think I may sell this house soon· The architect for planning permission came round to see me and is appealing for the plans to be passed and is

quite sure they will be. We will know in a week and then I can choose my period cottage in the country – How I will love that. . . ."

It would have been useful to have outline planning permission for a few houses on our plot as that would have raised the value of it.

My mother, who had always loved the countryside felt a bit hemmed in. She was finding the old house was getting too big. Gilbert was in the navy and was seldom home and Peter was becoming successful as a pop musician. John too was doing well in his career as an electronics engineer and Michael was soon to leave school. The main reason for a change was financial: the rates payable on the house were high and it was expensive to maintain but with house values rising it was a good time to sell. So it was in 1964 we started to look for a house in the country. Chessington Cottage was put on the market and we hoped it might sell to another large family. Sadly however, like others around, it was sold for redevelopment.

Chessington Cottage back garden in spring 1964

The Move to the Surrey Countryside

While in Worcester Park, Zou Zou loved the house and garden and the space it gave her for the five children to live in. I suppose that it also reminded her of Bart and that always made her sad. She longed to live in the countryside. She loved the little cottages in rural Surrey. Granada had lived briefly in a cottage in Shamley Green and then had moved "Primrose Cottage" in Ewhurst - which was left to her and her sisters in Gladys' will – but she felt lonely and isolated there so moved back to Shamley Green to live with Billie and Graham. Mother envied them the access to the woodland walks and the pretty surroundings and grew increasingly dissatisfied with suburban Greater London.

As the boys left school she was proud that Gilbert had achieved his ambition of becoming a clearance diver, John had an electronics apprenticeship with Decca and Peter was a pop musician. She listened avidly to the radio to hear the Overlanders and wrote to all the request shows and bought the Melody Maker and the NME. In many ways she had fewer worries now that the three boys were doing so well. Now she considered what is currently called "downsizing". The house was expensive to run and the garden was getting hard for her to keep up so she put the house on the market.

Moving meant a huge clearout. The house had six bedrooms, four reception rooms plus scullery, two bathrooms, pantry, greenhouse, cellars, large sheds and a garage. She was moving to a smaller-scale house altogether. Old papers were burnt on the bonfire. I saw her throw my father's love letters onto the flames, but she said they only made her sad and she wanted the move to be a new beginning, so we watched them burn.

She was not feeling as well as before, and she was having periods every two weeks having had a monthly cycle that was as regular as clockwork all her life. The doctors told her that she must have a hysterectomy and it was organised quite quickly. She went to St Bartholomew's Hospital (where her name caused some amusement). They told her she might be anaemic and, if so, she would need to get us to bring in stout and Guinness for her to drink. She was disappointed when her blood tests showed otherwise.

After the operation she was sent for a week's convalescence at Elstead. I remember Gilbert driving us down there to visit her. On the way back he bought a pound of local Cheddar cheese. Ever since I had started school at the age of five, and had been forced to eat rectangles of processed cheese in salads there, I had refused to eat raw cheese. I tried this one because I was told it was good and I knew that I shouldn't make a fuss if

Gilbert and John were being good enough to cater for us. I was amazed at how nice it was and started eating cheese again at the age of fourteen.

We looked at cottages in Hampshire, Surrey and Sussex and finally found a period tile-hung cottage with black oak beams and a third of an acre garden and a large barn. It dated from 1540. (We were told that a cottage on the site is noted in the Doomsday book.) This was "Chilston Cottage" on Church Road in Milford.

Chilston Cottage, by Zou Zou

We sold Chessington Cottage to the Tucker family next door and they sold both properties for development. We moved in September 1964 using Messenger's Removals. I was surprised, when we had packed the three vans, that Mrs Messenger turned up in a car with Christine and Theresa, the twins I had gone to primary school with – I hadn't realised that it was their father's company. They said goodbye and wished us luck in our new home.

Mother celebrated her 53rd birthday in Milford soon after we moved. She was still convalescing from her operation. She loved her new home and the life in the village where she quickly made friends by joining the WI and the Guildford Cage Bird Club.

She had a lot of energy to make the garden and house as she wanted it. She bought a flowery Axminster carpet for the stairs which had a rich, almost yellow background which filled the hall with sunshine on the dullest of days.

Upstairs corridor with carpet

Below:
Back of the cottage

She removed some plaster and boarding to reveal a bread oven and some beams and had the rooms decorated in white with a hint of other colours. Since then the idea was taken up by the paint companies for their large selection of coloured off-white paints.

In the inglenook we had a blazing log and coal fire which warmed most of the house. One day, when the fire was going, I noticed a bad smell during lunch – it was like hot varnish. Neither Michael nor Mother was worried by it. Later Michael went to practise his clarinet in the dining room and noticed a wisp of smoke coming from the chimneybreast there. I called the fire brigade and they came quickly and put out a fire in the main chimney without making too much mess. However, soon after they had gone we saw it had reignited and we called them back. This time they put down sheets and removed the false ceiling of the inglenook to reveal the smouldering beam. This time they made sure that the fire was extinguished.

The inglenook

The ceiling plate had been put in at the level of a beam and soot against it had set the beam itself alight. When it was repaired, we put it back higher up where this could not happen again. Mother took this in her stride; she was fascinated by the view up the unrestricted chimney which had hooks for hanging and smoking meat.

Outside she converted the garage into an aviary and had Fella, her lesser Indian mynah, and lots of other birds there. She joined a local bird club and went on trips and to shows to see the best in foreign birds. She won some rosettes and small prizes for her birds and bred Java Sparrows and Chinese Painted Quail. She also put up a dovecot and had a few tumbler pigeons that were a delight to watch as they sped through the sky doing their aerobatic displays.

Once when she was waiting for a bus in Farncombe just beyond Godalming, some children pulled a long twig off the weeping willow beside the bus stop and then threw it down. She took it home and stuck it in beside our pond where it grew into a very nice little tree.

The barn had an earth floor, old oak beams and was weather-boarded. There were advertising hoardings all along the front which Mother had removed. She had a builder come to brick up between the beams add a balcony at the end and put in a sprung floor. She was then able to use the barn as a studio and completed several miniatures there. The council insisted that the roadside wall remained weather-boarded as it was a listed building, so it was a mystery to us that the hoardings had ever been allowed.

She painted some watercolours of birds and took them to a shop in Godalming where they hung them on the wall for sale. She sold one or two but it was not very remunerative.

It was around this time that Graham's elder brother Reggie died. Graham put a notice in the Times saying that Reginald, eldest grandson of Duncombe, Earl of Feversham in Yorkshire, had died. Graham and his siblings were the children of a second marriage, following a childless divorce. The old Earl had not accepted this and had disowned his son and any offspring. However, the Earldom was vacant and the nearest other relative was a South African. The press and the people of Feversham took this up and Graham and Billie visited Yorkshire.

Graham might have taken on the title but he had no son of his own to inherit from him. Conveniently he was then offered the position of Military Knight of Windsor- the equivalent of the Beefeaters at the Tower of London. This is a retirement job given to the best of retired senior military ranks. Field Marshal Slim, who had been Graham's senior officer in Burma, was a Knight of Windsor. The position carried with it a house in the walls of Windsor Castle for the rest of your life and, while able, you had to appear in uniform for Royal occasions and sometimes act as a guide around St George's

Chapel. It was what Graham and Billie had always hoped for but it was not available to lords, only to commoners! Graham therefore happily gave up the Feversham claim and they moved to Windsor.

They couldn't take 80-year-old Granada with them. She, meanwhile, had suffered a number of minor strokes. Mother agreed to have her at Milford.

It was a difficult time. Although most of the time she seemed alright, Granada was sometimes confused and got angry. She wandered around after Mother who felt guilty when she was irritated by it. She was also partially incontinent and had a habit of falling out of bed at night. Her health was steadily declining but I can't remember any real help that we received from doctors or other services. In 1966 looking after her became too difficult as her dementia was getting worse; she moved to a nursing home in Wormley where she died in October of that year just a month before her 83rd birthday.

Mother told me later "*I always regret that I didn't really understand how ill she was. I wish I could have been kinder to her and looked after her better. I only realised in retrospect that she had had those strokes.*" I know I too was rather unsympathetic.

Mother and I got on extremely well and even though I was a teenager we never quarrelled – except once that I remember: I don't know what we argued about but I left for school in a black mood. That evening it wasn't mentioned but she gave me a present of two drawing pencils. Neither of us said sorry but we didn't need to.

Two miniatures: one in oils from just before we left Worcester Park, and one done in 1970 in the barn studio.

In the late 1960s John, Gilbert and Peter all got married. John had been living with us in Milford but he and Jen bought a house in Dorking. Gilbert had met Sue in Cornwall while he was in the Royal Navy. He had 'signed on' for several years in order to work as a clearance diver and had loved the work, but he left the navy hoping to use his skills outside. Although he got work on the North Sea oil rigs he was unhappy with the lack of safety precautions and Sue encouraged him to give it up and try something else.

Meanwhile Peter had met Lis, a psychiatrist, and they were living in London. Then the Overlanders broke up (as with many groups it was due to arguments over finances). Mother liked and admired Lis but was in awe of her - she was so clever, so well qualified and so sure of herself. Tragedy struck in 1968 when Lis, who was pregnant, became very ill with ulcerative colitis and she died that July.

Mother's first grand-daughters were born that autumn – Lucinda on the day before Mother's birthday and Anna Elisabeth (called Lis) on the day after her 33rd wedding anniversary.

Gilbert and Sue and baby Lucinda moved into Chilston Cottage briefly while Gilbert found work locally. This was difficult for Mother as she didn't see eye to eye with her daughter-in-law. I can still picture her literally biting her lip! However, she really loved looking after and getting to know her eldest grandchild.

When finally in 1969 I left to go to university in Cardiff, Mother was alone for the first time. I phoned her and wrote letters weekly, but I vowed not to be homesick and didn't come home at all during term time. Only now do I see that I should perhaps have come back for her sake. John and Gilbert were both living some distance away and busy with work, home and children. They seldom visited. Michael was studying in London and living with the widowed Peter (and by that time with Jeanette).

There were opportunities to paint and she often took photos of interesting local buildings in order to draw or paint them. She tried her hand at illustration and Christmas cards. Although she had made friends of many neighbours in Milford and had joined the W.I. giving her a reasonable social life, she was still lonely despite busying herself with painting and with her birds.

Christmas cards by Zou Zou Bartholomew

Witley Church and Steps Cottage

The Ram Inn
Godalming   Z E Bartholomew
                                    1969

She did try to investigate different religions. She believed in Christianity and God but she could not take any kind of dogmatic or pious stance seriously. She made friends with a Quaker and went to some of their services. She said there were long silences and people speaking out their thoughts and she couldn't bring herself to join in; it was all rather tense and slightly embarrassing. One of her new friends was the mother of Roger Taylor, the drummer in the pop group Queen.

There was a spiritualist church in Godalming and she found that interesting. She said the services were fascinating but she did wonder how many Red Indians there were and why so many were spirit guides! She felt there was a lot of truth in it and that some spiritual healers had a gift. Having experienced ghostly activity in Andover, she wanted to believe that spirits of the dead could send messages but found herself sceptical of much of what went on there.

A Jehovah's Witness visited. Mother told her categorically that she could not believe it was right to withhold a blood transfusion from someone who needed it. She allowed the woman to talk to her but showed her distrust of fundamentalism. The woman was friendly so Mother agreed to go to the church to some of their services. When she continued to reject some of their dogmas they left her alone again. I used to return from school to discuss religious points with her and I think any progress the Witness had made was obliterated in our discussions. She told me that the woman's son had left school but had not bothered to get any training or a job because he believed it wasn't worth it in the time from then until Armageddon. He's still waiting.

While I was at school she decided to get a job to get extra money. She had no qualifications so took a job at the Lake Hotel in Godalming as a chambermaid. There she worked with another woman who became a good friend. It was a feature of Zou Zou's character that she had no problems with class; she was happy to take on this menial work without a second thought. She was the same talking to a Lord or a gypsy because she genuinely believed that goodness of character overrode any accident of birth. She also hated wastefulness and the job kept us in small, green, slightly-used soaps for a long time.

Briefly she had a boyfriend called George. He came to survey the house for woodworm. There was a good deal of both woodworm and death-watch beetle in the ancient beams but he told her that they were beyond danger and having lasted for 400 years they would probably outlast her. He visited her regularly for a few months and she became quite fond of him but I believe he was married and nothing came of it.

In 1970, at the age of 59, Zou Zou learnt to drive a car. She bought Peter's cream and red Mini from him. She was a very cautious driver and it wasn't easy for her to learn or to get enough practice. She ended up taking the test five times and each time she would come out in hives beforehand through nervousness. Finally she did pass and it opened up new horizons for her, giving her much more freedom and control of her time.

Sometimes she would visit the local antique/junk shops with local friends, Mr and Mrs Olive, and bought herself some objets d'art.

Mother had visits from her cousin, Gladys Smedley and from Grace Sjobek, Mary's sister, while she lived in Milford. Finally Mary (Sjobek) Evans and her husband, John, came to visit us. It was the first time they had met since childhood but photos, letters and presents had been sent regularly.

Zou Zou with Mary and Elizabeth in about 1972

One day, while she was gardening near the back of the cottage, she lost her wedding ring. She had worn it ever since 1935 and when she moved house she told the new owners that it must still be somewhere in the garden. A long time later they called her: they had found her ring and were able to return it to her.

Apple Tree – by Zou Zou - and John in OU graduation robes

Chilston Cottage was her favourite house. She told me later, when she was ill, that she wished she had stayed there as it had been her ideal house and she had been very happy there.

Witley

Any profits that she had made on the sale of Worcester Park and the purchase of Chilston Cottage were gradually used up. She now found the rates at Milford quite high and decided to live in a simpler, smaller house. She found a pretty little tile-hung Victorian cottage in Little London, a lane off Gasden Lane in Witley. It was semi-detached with a long, rather overgrown garden and a garage. It was built of the local, slightly yellow sandstone and had two bedrooms and a bathroom upstairs and one reception room and a kitchen downstairs. The rates and running costs were less and it had the advantage of being adjacent to Mare Hill where she liked to walk almost every day.

Mare Hill was a sandy bit of common land with heather and some small trees. One part had an area where sundews grew. The usual path we took when I visited led to the road and over into Witley Common or to Milford Common where the nightingales could still be heard in the 1970s.

The house was big enough for her needs and the move released a bit of capital to smooth the finances. Also in 1971 she reached state pension age and her investment in National

Insurance stamps had at last paid off. She was able to trade the car in for a new purple mini at the end of the "K" registration (1973).

She told me that it seemed strange to be a pensioner because inside she felt exactly the same as she had when she was seventeen.

She tried some "Lonely Hearts" adverts and made friends with a vet from Peckham in London. He called himself Bill Williams and would visit and enjoy walks across the common with Zou Zou. He invited Mother and me to visit him in London where, from the brass plate we found his name was actually Bill Angel. I think he found that name an embarrassment! He was a cheerful man and visited regularly and she enjoyed his company. He also gave the old cat her injections for free!

Puddy (the feral cat we gave a home to in Milford) and Pao Pei aged 15 in Witley.

Pao Pei died at the age of 16 and Mother now had just the aviary of birds and the old mother cat, Puddy, whom we had given a home when she was a stray with kittens in Milford. One day a gentleman was passing the gate and his dog chased Puddy into the back garden. He apologised and introduced himself and his dog, Cleo the golden Labrador. He was Bill Auxenfans.

Bill lived in Tudor Cottage at the corner of Little London. He was a widower and a keen gardener. He retained the title of "Major" having been in the army, but most of his career had been as an accountant. He had lived in a succession of nice houses which he had improved and then sold at a profit and he was therefore "comfortably off".

Tudor Cottage by Zou Zou

Bill was able to give Zou Zou a new social life. She went to dinner with his friends and visited places with him. They went for walks over the common with the dog. It was nice for Zou to have his companionship. He maintained a military air and was very conservative to the extent that her name, Zou, unsettled him and he took to calling her 'Sue' on the pretext that it made little difference. For her part, she had always been adaptable and mutable so she was glad of his company.

Bill had two daughters. Anne (married to an architect Cedric Kitchin) had three children, Nolly (Down's syndrome), Matthew and Sophie. Liz (married to Brian Quance) had two sons, Julian and Miles. When Bill proposed marriage to Mother, both his daughters warned her that he could be unreasonable, difficult and even unkind. They said that, when their mother had been ill with cancer, he had not been as understanding or supportive as he should have been, but rather intolerant. We now have the expression "controlling husband" to describe his character.

She told me: "Dulcie has had Geoff, who was the love of her life, since she was 17, but her reaction when I told her about Bill amazed me." When she told her sister that she was thinking of marrying again, Dulcie's reaction was: "But don't you still love Bart?" Mother was horrified (because of course she did) but her sister didn't seem to realise how alone she had been: "He has been dead these 25 years!" she pointed out.

Mother told me that Bill had asked her to marry him and asked me which Bill, Auxenfans or Angel, did I prefer. I told her I liked Bill Angel! I think, if he had also spoken of marriage, she might have had more trouble deciding. She accepted Bill Auxenfans and they were married on 1st February 1975.

Marriage meant moving to Tudor Cottage. She sold Wildcroft Cottage for about £12,000. Rather than her having a stake in Tudor Cottage, it remained in Bill's name and her money was invested. They kept their money quite separate. Puddy, as adaptable as her mistress, moved happily to live with Cleo and an aviary was constructed by the summerhouse in the garden.

Having downsized twice already, she had honed her belongings to things that had good associations and that meant a lot to her. However, she had then to do it again. Bill helped her and moved a lot of stuff, that "would have to go", to the garage. Martin and I saved a Japanese red lacquer tray with a picture of two Samurai on it from the rubbish pile. Bill had folded it in half to get it into a rubbish sack. Mother urged us to take anything we liked or thought we could use.

For some time Mother was happy. They had a holiday in the Canary Isles – only her second foreign holiday during my lifetime! Despite her natural fear of flying she had a lovely holiday in Madeira and particularly enjoyed the amazing flora on the island.

Bill was both a Roman Catholic and a smoker. His smoking gave him a rough voice and this became more and more broken and growly. Mother insisted that he go to the doctor because, she said, his voice was not healthy any more. Reluctantly he did so. The doctors diagnosed a throat cancer and he was sent for radio-therapy, which luckily saved his voice and his life. He was recuperating as Lent started and so gave up smoking at the start of Lent and never smoked again. Ironically having smoked most of his life, he became highly intolerant of smokers.

She soon found that Bill was rather a skinflint. He also criticised her use of her own money. She had always been generous particularly to her children and grandchildren. She learnt to keep such things secret from him: she lent money to me to buy a better car and we paid her back monthly, but she swore us to secrecy saying she would never hear the end of it if Bill were to find out.

- with Geoff Larkins

Grandpa Bill talking to Hugh

She also learnt not to argue over religion or politics with him. I remember her more or less warning me when we visited: "*We t*hink Margaret Thatcher is a wonderful Prime Minister, don't you?" she said!

While she was in Tudor Cottage she found some time to paint. She did a sketch of a boy who I think was Miles Quance and another which may have been Sophie Kitchen. She exhibited at least two miniatures, probably at The Society of Miniaturists in London, and Gwen went to see them.

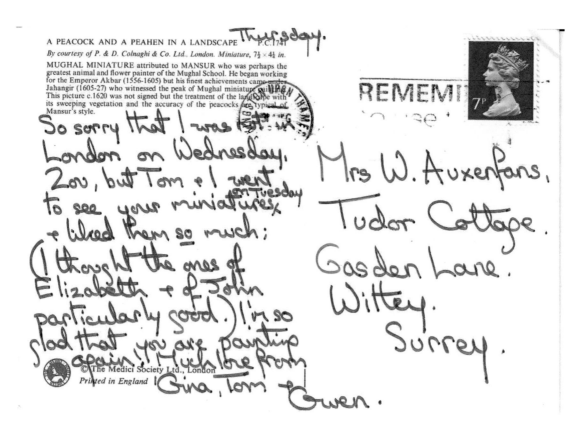

She still loved the visits from her grandchildren and soon after Zoë was born she spent ten days with me.

Zou Zou with Graham

Bill could be charming but she found him hard going sometimes. While she was well she seemed able to deal with him and get around him. He was not the soul-mate she had hoped for and I think despite the companionship and no longer having money worries, she still found herself lonely sometimes.

Tea at Tudor Cottage

It was in 1983 that "Leprechauns", a bungalow on the edge of the wood, came up for sale. They knew the owners and had admired it. It was well insulated, modern and convenient. Bill persuaded her that it would be a good move and he sold Tudor Cottage and bought it.

They moved house and again many more of their possessions had to go. Martin and I visited them with the children a week after the move. The place was immaculately tidy. Bill proudly told us that they had got everything unpacked and in place in two days. Mother said it had been very tiring but nice now to have it sorted. She enjoyed seeing the children and they were very well behaved. Zoë, the youngest of her 13 grandchildren, was just starting to walk a few steps while hanging onto the furniture.

Sophie (?) unfinished

The last years.

Shortly after their move to "Leprechauns" in early 1983, Zou was taken ill. She went into the kitchen one evening to get a hot water bottle ready for bed and there she collapsed. She was taken to hospital where they initially said she had had a minor stroke. However, she had also cracked her skull on the solid floor.

She was awake and responding but fell into a coma that lasted a couple of days. The injury had bled more and the result seemed to be that a massive stroke had followed the first. When she woke she was unable to use her left side. She could talk and we hoped that her movement would return. She was thankful that her right hand still functioned and hoped that she would still be able to write and to draw when she recovered.

Recovery was very slow. She eventually was moved from Guildford to the little hospital at Hydestile, which was little more than a collection of old army huts. She was in a wheel-chair and was encouraged to do exercises and to try to stand with help. She looked forward to getting better and said perhaps she would buy another car and drive again. It looked unlikely as she was hemiplegic and as time went on there was no real improvement, but we told her we hoped so and that she must keep doing the exercises that the physiotherapist had suggested.

She returned home to be nursed by Bill with help from carers every morning and evening. It was not a success. She told me she was actually scared of Bill because he got so exasperated with her. She spent a few weeks with Peter and his family and then with us in Bristol.

The right side of the brain controls the left side of the body and also is used in the interpretation of vision. When stroke affects the areas of the brain that process the visual information, it can cause 'visual neglect' (lack of awareness to one half of the body or space) as well as difficulties with judging depth and movement. Presented with a plate of food, although she seemed to be able to see all around her, she would eat everything on the right side of the plate and leave the rest. She was amazed when we turned the plate around 180 degrees and more food appeared. Her visual confusion also meant that she couldn't read anything that she wrote and nor could she draw any more, which she found frustrating and distressing. During that time with us she seemed to be doing well.

Bristol NHS arranged for her to go to a centre where there were activities designed to encourage her.

Finally Bill got her into a nursing home in Midhurst where he could visit her regularly and so could all her family. There, sadly, she declined. Any hopes of recovery were soon lost and she became gradually less mobile. The less she did while awake and the more time she spent asleep dreaming, the more confused she became between reality and dreams. She died there on 12th December 1987 aged 76.

In the playground near Carron House Nursing Home in Midhurst. 1985 - with Graham, Zoë, Hugh and Elizabeth.

Zou Zou's legacy is great. She was the mother of five, with 13 grandchildren, five step-grandchildren. She is the great-grandmother of one American girl, two New Zealanders and fifteen English children. She would have loved them all, wept for their sorrows and celebrated their successes.

Her funeral was at the Roman Catholic Church in Milford and she was cremated and her ashes were scattered at the Crematorium in Compton.

Bill lived a few years more but the cancer reappeared in his jaw and he died in August 1990.

There remain pictures and portraits that she painted and drawings she made. It is good to think that, in this way, part of her lives on. Perhaps her main achievements will never be obvious; they are there in the way she influenced us and in our fond memories of her.